Making Pet Houses, Carriers
& Other Projects

Charles R. Self

Sterling Publishing Co., Inc.   New York

Acknowledgments

Much help was received from David Draves at Woodcraft, as well as Stan Black, President of Trend-Lines. Georgia-Pacific's Janet Folk helped with materials. Kim Park of Porter-Cable was generous with both time and tools for photographs. Makita's Roy Thompson, and Ryobi's Jim Ippolito also provided invaluable assistance, as did John Butler of Black & Decker's auto division (which distributes shop vacuums) in reducing a dust problem with my Delta table saw.

Stanley Tools, through Mike Isser (Isser & Assoc.) and Fran Hummel was a help. CooperTools, through Richard Ziff, also provided help, as did American Clamping Corporation, distributors of Mifer chisels and Bessey clamps.

AMT provided a tool that widened my outlook on woodworking, a heavy duty lathe, while David Draves made getting reaccustomed to the work easier with a set of Sorby HSS chisels that cut maple as if it were cheese.

Help with finishes was provided by Joe Gibbons at UGL (makers of ZAR products), and help with glues by Franklin Chemical Industries.

Dub and Bert Jones provided photographs and shared their concept of elevated, deck-style dog pens.

Marvin Becker helped a great deal in picking up measurements and reproducing the plans for the American Plywood Association's Gambrel Roofed Doghouse. The APA had the idea and the photograph, but had lost the plans and measurements.

Of great help was Bobby Weaver, a friend who is also a woodworker, and whose hands appear in many of the photographs.

Front and back cover inset photographs of doghouses with dogs courtesy of the American Plywood Association, Tacoma, WA.

Edited and layout designed by
Rodman Pilgrim Neumann

Library of Congress Cataloging-in-Publication Data

Self, Charles R.
    Making pet houses, carriers & other projects / by Charles R. Self.
        p.   cm.
    Includes index.
    ISBN 0-8069-7248-3
    1. Pets—Housing—Design and construction. I. Title.
SF414.2.S45 1991
690'.89—dc20   90-47871
                                                      CIP

10 9 8 7 6 5 4 3 2 1

Contents

Introduction

You may have a number of reasons for wanting to construct doghouses, cat homes, cat toys, dog or cat carriers, and various accessories in your home shop: The variation in both sizes and styles is far greater than that available already built, and, with some care, if it is your aim, a good deal of money can be saved.

A particular animal's size needs can also be easily suited when building a home-shop version: my plans, and those from others, are all sized, but any of them can be adjusted to fit your pet's requirements. Simply increase (or decrease, if desired) one dimension, and make a rough drawing on tracing paper to see how the other dimensions are affected. The changes should be proportional, the same relationship holding for each dimension. Then increase (or decrease, as appropriate) those dimensions correspondingly.

I hope you enjoy the plans included here, but first we must all keep safety foremost by reminding ourselves of a few home-shop safety pointers.

Woodworking Safety

Safety when working with wood is something we all aim for. We remove watches and jewelry, keep our clothing from flapping and catching in tools, and so on.

It is in the woodworking techniques, though—even after all basic shop safety rules are met—that we may run into significant safety problems. Woodworking is inherently dangerous. It is a business or hobby that requires our constant attention to safety to maintain our full complement of digits, and other appendages.

I have tried to make all techniques, and plans, described as safe as possible, assuming they are handled with reasonable care. If at any point you feel uncomfortable with a technique or a design, do not use that technique or design. If a design seems essential, but feels dangerous to you, modify it, or its work requirements, until it feels safe.

What is safe in my shop may not be safe in yours, and vice versa. Working techniques and emotional state all impinge on safety, along with some strength and physical conditioning requirements. Each of us differs. Thus, in the end, it is you who must make the decision as to safety. No matter how something is described, it is impossible for me to even envision, never mind cover, all the various ways a described method or device may be changed to fit your circumstances.

Keep it safe for you.

Charlie Self

1
Woods and Other Materials for Pet Housing

Wood is a natural material ideally suited for construction: it can be bent or shaped with tools (Illus. 1.1), and it is durable when subject to abrasion or to different stresses. Certain kinds are durable under weathering

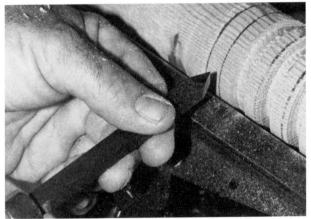

Illus. 1.1 *Wood is machinable using any of a wide range of tools, such as this lathe.*

Illus. 1.2 *Preparing to cut a 5-inch hole in plywood, this drill will work well, but it's really far better to use a drill press.*

conditions that would ruin many materials, including steel. Wood is also relatively inexpensive while possessing an inherent beauty.

For larger projects with wide flat expanses of wood, plywood is especially suitable, typically allowing the entire project to be cut from a single sheet (Illus. 1.2). Standard construction lumber is useful for projects that require internal bracing. Several projects also allow the use of better grades of softwoods and hardwoods (Illus. 1.3).

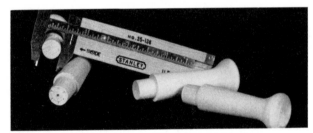

Illus. 1.3 *The pegs are of hardwood birch.*

Milling

The common methods of milling a tree are sawing around the board, and sawing through the board. Both produce flat grain boards (Illus. 1.4). Sawing directly through the tree as it is fed into the sawmill, with no changes in tree position, tends to produce a mix of figures.

Flat-sawn lumber is not the best for precise woodworking because it mixes sapwood and heartwood and approaches edge grain at the board edges (Illus. 1.5). The different densities and drying needs of the sap-

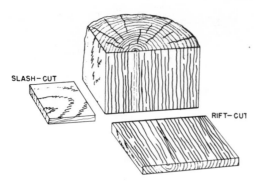

Illus. 1.4 Standard milling of a log.

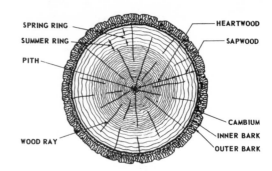

Illus. 1.5 Cross section of a tree.

wood and heartwood mean that the board will warp and cup. The wider the board, the worse the cupping. Flat-sawn lumber can be identified by the U- or V-shaped markings at the ends of the boards.

Quarter-sawn lumber is cut generally at a 90° angle to the growth rings (Illus. 1.6), but it costs more than flat sawn. There is less of a mix of heartwood and sapwood in each board, so less tendency to warp and cup. As the first step in quarter sawing, the log is fed through the mill to cut it in half. Each half is in turn cut in half, forming four sections, or quarters. The quarters are then cut from the outsides in, giving a radial section that produces parallel line patterns of wood grain.

Rotary cutting, or peeling, of logs is used for basic plywoods. More costly veneers use half-round slicing, or quarter slicing. Quarter slicing is analogous to quarter sawing, but in this case a knife takes a very thin—often as little as 1/28th of an inch thick—slice off the quarter of wood. Slicing produces less waste than sawing.

Before you begin a project, take a look at the general run of woods to see what is both the best and the most economical for that particular application.

Plywood

In earlier years plywood received, and often deserved, something of a bum rap. Ply separation was the usual problem. However, by World War II certain types were well-enough made to allow their use in small boats (PT boats were of plywood construction). While marine plywoods are of

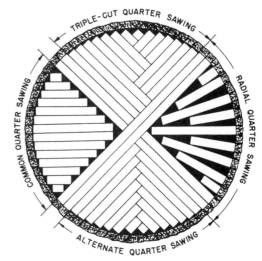

Illus. 1.6 Four methods of quarter sawing.

little or no use for these pet-home projects, a number of exterior and interior grades are helpful. "Exterior" or "interior" is a broad classification that originated in 1930 when the first waterproof phenol formaldehyde adhesive was used, creating the distinction.

Softwood plywood grading standards are uniform for members of the American Plywood Association (APA) and start with face grades. Face grades vary from A to C, for these pet-home projects.

A is a sanded panel face, suitable for painting or staining. A-A grade, available in interior or exterior plywood, is made with minimum grade D interior filler plies for the interior grade and C interior for the exterior and is suitable for situations where both faces will show. A-B has a second face not as good as the A face, but still smooth and suitable for painting. Again, exterior and interior A-B grades are made, but with A-C only an exterior type is made whereas A-D is produced only in an interior grade.

B grades work down in a manner similar to A grades, starting with a face ply that is less free of defects (Illus. 1.7). B grades are generally considered suitable for uses in which the surfaces will be painted or covered with other materials.

C grades are usually unsanded and often have open spots in the face ("C-C Plugged" has most of those openings filled and may also be called "underlayment" grade). C-C is the lowest grade you can buy in exterior plywood grades, and is suitable for many kinds of rough work, including sheathing. C-D is an interior rough-construction type, but made with exterior glues. Sometimes called CDX, it is not useful for permanent outdoor installation.

Oriented strand board (OSB) is described as wood panels made from reconstituted, mechanically oriented wood strands that are bonded with resins, under heat and pressure. The strands are laid up in layers, at right angles to each other. OSB may be a single panel, or the middle layer in other panels. Waferboard is a similar product, made from wood wafers instead of strands. The wafers are not directionally oriented (Illus. 1.8). Waferboard and OSB may qualify as a performance board for sheathing and various other duties.

A fairly new face veneer grade, N, offers a natural finish veneer and may be all heartwood, or all sapwood, according to your specification when you order it. Any repairs—limited by definition to six per panel—must be made parallel to the grain and match for grain and color. This is the most costly grade of softwood plywood.

The species of wood used for the plywood face is important only in how it affects your finish. In truth, softwood plywood isn't that pretty when stained, so a painted surface is probably best. If a natural finish is desired, low-grade solid pine is probably no more expensive than pine-faced plywood. Fir is slightly more costly.

Plywood is laid up in odd-number plies; thin ⅛-inch and ¼-inch sheets have three plies, ⅜-inch and ½-inch plywood have five plies, and so on. The thickness of each ply

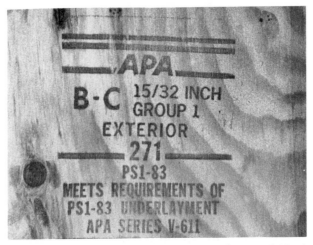

Illus. 1.7 APA (American Plywood Association) grade stamp on Georgia-Pacific B-C exterior grade plywood.

Illus. 1.8 Waferboard being cut for a project.

changes as plywood thickness changes. For most uses, you will rarely see more than seven plies, though some types have as many as 15. Sheets, or panels, are available in four-foot widths with lengths ranging from eight to 12 feet—some may be special-ordered longer.

Various wood species are used for softwood plywood interior plies, some softwood, some hardwood. Typical hardwood species are aspen, the softer maples, cottonwood, basswood, or similar hardwoods, however, some may actually be beech, birch, sugar (hard or rock) maple, lauan, or sweetgum. The lower the group number—there are five—the stiffer and stronger the plywood. So look for Group 1 or 2 when strength and stiffness are important.

Plywood serves best where panel strength is a requisite. However, large doghouses may need some internal bracing in the form of two-by-three or two-by-four framing. Nevertheless most doghouses can readily be constructed of plywood, with medium-sized versions made of ¾-inch thickness, with no internal bracing (Illus. 1.9). By the same token, almost any kind of cat home can be made of ⅝-inch, ½-inch, or even ⅜-inch plywood, OSB, or waferboard.

The use of plywood in some form doesn't necessarily rule out the use of solid woods: for large pet houses, plywood may be used as sheathing, which is covered with solid wood used as siding. For super-fancy doghouses and other pet houses, internal framing—and even separate rooms—may be delineated in much the same manner as are human houses. This is done with two-by-four or two-by-three framing, various types of plywood, and various types of drywall. One project for a large doghouse of that sort (see page 74) is presented as an adaptation of a smaller unit. However, I don't recommend spoiling dogs; the effect is the same as with children.

Hardwood plywood is different in form and intended use from softwood plywood. Whereas softwood plywood is generally less costly and most often meant for general construction projects, hardwood plywood is most often used for cabinetry and furniture. The face ply species tend to be the more attractive hardwoods, including white oak, red oak, birch, cherry, walnut, teak as well as many others, but seldom such species as alder, aspen, or poplar.

Edging Plywoods

Covering the raw edges of plywood is one of the first indications of a neat woodworking job. There are now a multitude of methods for this, some simple, some difficult.

Edge-banding of hardwood plywoods is a recent "hot" method, in which real wood edge-banding is added using a machine to glue it in place. Other forms of edge-banding are made with a glue backing—the

Illus. 1.9 Inside of a project made of plywood. Note best face of plywood is up for the floor on which the animal will rest.

one I use most involves a simple 250-foot coil of real wood. This is unfurled, placed and cut against the edge to be covered. Then a standard home iron is run over the front of the band, melting the glue and providing a good, tight edge cover. Other types of edge-banding involve simple straight strips, either with or without glue, which may be installed (in the glue-free models) with any form of adhesive, including contact cement which requires no clamping. If you use regular adhesives, clamping may be necessary: use 2-inch wide masking tape to clamp the edge-band to the structure, at 12-inch intervals.

Of course, cutting a mitre on each corner automatically covers the raw edges when the pieces are joined. This is generally a simple process if your table saw is equipped with an aftermarket fence, and if you have an accurate blade angle set up. Otherwise, it can drive you nuts. My table saw has an Excalibur fence, which greatly simplifies the cutting of long edge mitres.

Solid-wood edging may also be used. This is cut to just a fraction oversize (for later sanding) compared to the thickness of the plywood, and then is glued in place. Contact cement is not really suitable for materials as thick as this, so either white or yellow glue should be used. That means clamping, which is best done with edge clamps (Illus. 1.10).

Illus. 1.10 Oak edging on B-C plywood goes on easily with glue and edge clamps.

Wood filler can also serve as an edge filler for plywood, especially when the edges will be painted. It is simple, fast, and inexpensive.

Solid Woods

Solid woods are specifically those woods that are sawn from a log and planed for later use. They may or may not be kiln or air dried to a particular moisture content, but they are not laminates, particleboards, or any other kind of manufactured wood products.

Softwoods are generally used as construction lumber (Illus. 1.11). Whereas, hardwoods are used for furniture and cabinetry. Though, as with most generalizations, these fall apart, since pine, fir, cedar, redwood, and other softwoods are used for furniture as well as in general construction.

Illus. 1.11 Softwood posts for a cat bed.

It's necessary to know a little about the grading of solid woods, so that the least costly and easiest-to-use wood with the greatest expected durability may be selected for each project.

Finish grade lumber is used where you desire the highest quality finish, particularly for stains and clear finishes.

Board grade lumber is used for sheathing, subflooring, shelving, boxing, and carting in general. This grade is probably the most generally useful for projects that require boards of any kind: when I refer to boards, I mean by that solid wood that is nominally 1 inch thick, or less.

Dimension lumber is surfaced softwood lumber for joists, rafters, studs, and small timbers. This is the most usual overall type of softwood solid wood lumber to be found these days. For building these pet-home projects, it is sufficient to know that dimension lumber comes in structural light framing, light framing, stud, structural joist, and plank styles. There is also an appearance framing grade.

Structural light framing grades fit applications where higher bending strength ratios are needed.

Light framing grades provide good appearance at design levels that do not require specially high strength.

Studs are suitable for all stud construction purposes.

Structural joists and planks are larger members that carry loads. Strength varies with grade.

Appearance grade has especially good appearance, combined with high strength.

Timber is applied to wood that is nominally five inches-by-five inches or larger and is used to carry loads.

Refer to the chart in Appendix B (page 124) that gives a listing of the main softwood lumber products, the grades available, and descriptions of each grade.

Remaining grades are for structural joists and planks, or for appearance framing. General softwood grading differs little from the above, though appearance grades are classed as Superior, Prime, E, and boards as No. 1 Common, down through No. 5 Common, with framing lumber starting at Select Structural (SS) No. 1, to SS No. 2, SS No. 3 (and the same for structural joists and planks, as well as timbers). Studs are simply classed as Studs.

As is almost always the case, especially with smaller projects, it is a good idea to check out lumber at the lumberyard: take the extra time to find a yard that will let you select your own lumber, piece by piece.

Hardwood Lumber

Hardwood lumber isn't as easy to come by, or as easy to buy as softwood lumber (Illus. 1.12 and 1.13). The costs begin at about two times as high on up—way, way up in the case of some exotics—but virtually always twice as high as any softwood (with the exception of redwood purchased in the eastern U.S., where the transportation costs tend to make the prices high).

Hardwood lumber is generally available in only four grades, which would seem to make selection easier, but there is usually more of a problem with matching grain, making sure the free cut lengths needed are available in such grain matches, and so on.

Outside of the four general grades, the grades set by the National Hardwood Lumber Association are slightly different for each species. I won't get into that here, but the four general grades used are : FAS (first and seconds); Select; No. 1 Common; No. 2 Common. FAS is the best, and most expensive, grade, for which pieces should be no less than six inches wide and eight feet long. At least 83⅓ percent of each board should provide clear cuttings. Selects gives the same amount of clear cutting in boards four inches wide and six feet long or longer. One face may have more defects than the other.

The two common grades should provide boards at least three inches wide by four feet long, with No. 1 Common giving 66⅔ percent clear cuttings, and No. 2 producing 50 percent.

Examining lumber for purchase, you will note some defects that are readily apparent. Some may not become obvious until later, when you may find internal knots and other faults that don't appear on the surfaces.

Wane is bark along the edges of the board, or missing wood along the edge of the board—usually caused by bark dropping off (Illus. 1.14).

Checking is splitting of the board, usually at the ends, but sometimes at other spots (Illus. 1.15).

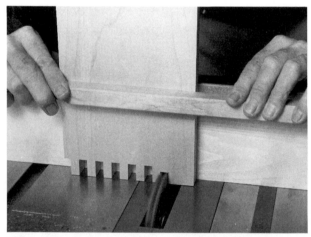

Illus. 1.12 Maple being finger-jointed for a cat resting box.

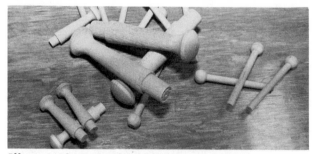

Illus. 1.13 Turned Shaker hardwood pegs in two sizes, along with tie/belt pegs.

Illus. 1.14 Wane.

Illus. 1.15 Checking and knots at the end of a one-by-twelve pine board ruin almost two board feet.

Illus. 1.16 A pitch pocket and knot in a sap-stained board—the sap stain is not as readily apparent, when reproduced in a black and white photo, but it is clearly visible in real life.

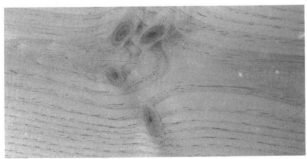

Illus. 1.17 Pin knots.

Cupping is warping of a board across its width, deviating from flatness.

Warping is a distortion of the shape of the wood, usually in combination of a linear twist and some cupping.

Crook is another form of warping, a deviation in the end-to-end straightness.

Crack is exactly that: a crack or large radial check (Illus. 1.15).

Diamonding is a form of warp, too—square sections of the board are distorted to a diamond shape and round sections become oval.

Sap stain is a bluish stain caused by fungi in the wood and on the surface (Illus. 1.16).

Knots are parts of branches which the expanding tree has overgrown. *Pin knots* are those knots less than a quarter inch in diameter (Illus. 1.17), while *spike knot* refers to any knot that has been cut along its long axis, giving its exposed section a stretched appearance. *Sound knots* are solid throughout the board and show no signs of rot, whereas *knotholes* are knots that are completely absent, leaving only a hole and the surrounding tree growth (Illus. 1.18).

Encased, or black, knots are knots that are loose, but remain in the tree, trapped by later growth (Illus. 1.19).

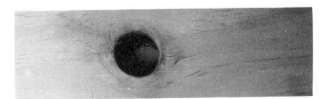

Illus. 1.18 Knothole.

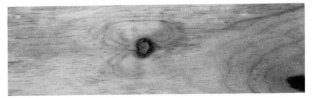

Illus. 1.19 Black knot.

Fasteners

Mechanical fasteners generally include anything from screws to nails and the range in between, with some variations. If the variation isn't in the design of the screws or nails, then it is in the devices to be used with them, such as bracing and mending plates.

Bracing and mending plates are simply flat metal plates that are screwed over a joint to brace that joint: they may be used to mend, but are just as often used on a new joint for bracing (Illus. 1.20). They come in Ts, Ls, Hs and a variety of other shapes that occasionally prove very useful (Illus. 1.21 and 1.22). New types appear regularly, as is the case with both nails and screws.

Changing Screw Designs. In recent years changes have leaned towards screw types that are meant to be power-driven. The array of cordless power-drivers now available has produced a need for screw-head designs that prevent the driver tip from twisting out of the slot or insert as power is applied. Such head designs are termed cam-out resisting. The cam-out problem is more likely with slotted screws. Currently, there's an emphasis on Phillips head and square insert screws for use with both hand- and power-drivers. The standard slotted head persists, but well in the background. All of the new screws are adapted for use with hand drivers as well as power-drivers. Thus there is no impediment to their use, while the cost differential is also very small.

Screw Types. Screws may be classified as wood screws, lag screws, or metal screws. Wood screws offer round, flat, and oval heads, whereas metal screws offer pan, flat, and round heads, as well as a variety of others of little or no interest here. Lag screws generally have square or hexagonal heads, with coarser screw threads than wood screws. Lag screws are also likely to come in larger sizes. Wood screws run up to a six-inch length, and No. 24 shaft size (diameter is indicated with a number which relates

Illus. 1.20 Flat braces.

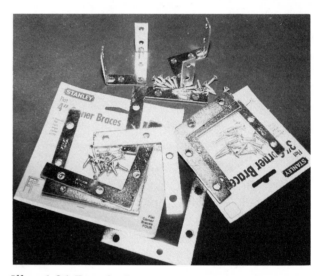

Illus. 1.21 Four-inch flat corner braces, 3-way corner braces (top), and three-inch flat corner braces.

Illus. 1.22 Five-inch L-shaped corner brace, available in a range of sizes up to about eight inches.

only indirectly to the actual fractional inch sizes). Commonly, you'll find wood screws up to about a four- or five-inch length and No. 16 size at most hardware dealers, in a number of materials. Most other sizes including extremely small sizes such as a quarter-inch length in the No. 0, 1, 2, or 3 sizes will have to be special-ordered.

Wood Screws. Wood screws may be made of mild steel, coated or uncoated, solid brass, or stainless steel. Coated types, and solid brass, are used where corrosion resistance is essential: a plated zinc or galvanized coating is normally used. Stainless steel screws are useful when corrosion problems run to extremes, such as on or around salt water and in high-acid environments. Steel screws are used where strength greater than that provided by brass screws is required. Brass screws are the weakest of the three generally available wood screw materials, however they are decorative and corrode very slowly. Stainless steel corrodes hardly at all, but is the most costly material. Mild steel, even when zinc-plated, is the cheapest material.

Wood screws come in standard sizes which vary from a quarter inch to six inches long, as mentioned above. For screws grading up to a one-inch length, the increase is by one-eighth-inch increments, whereas screws from one inch to three inches long increase by quarter-inch increments. Screws from three inches to six inches jump by half-inch increments. Shaft diameters vary according to the number used to specify such size. These numbers are arbitrary in that they don't correspond directly to any real measure, but they do rise with increasing size.

Power-drive screws, both fine- and coarse-threaded, come in sizes somewhat different than those used for the commonly available standard wood screws whose origins lie well in the past. Drive screws tend to be available in longer lengths relative to the shaft size—up to three inches with a No. 6 and seldom larger than a No. 9 shaft where common wood screws would be at least No.

Illus. 1.23 Trend-lines square-recess power-drive screws.

10, but most often No. 12, and frequently as thick as No. 14 (Illus. 1.23).

Power-drive screws currently available have a Phillips head or a square-recess drive head. They are exceptionally useful for such things as installing decking, wallboard, and wall panelling of certain types and for general light-construction duties like those involved in building some of the pet housing projects.

Screws are less economical than nails, but they do provide some benefits for the extra cost. Holding strength is much higher. Disassembly is easier, and nondestructive.

Screws, however, take more work to install. For many screws, a pilot hole is enough, but for flat-head wood screws, countersinking is essential. Flat-head wood screws, in particular, are used where screws are not meant to show, for decorative purposes, and are often counterbored. The resulting hole is filled with a plug that may be flush with the surface or domed.

When drilling pilot holes, keep the bit at least one size smaller than the screw shaft for hardwood, and two sizes smaller for softwood. Make the hole a half to two-thirds as deep as the screw will sink.

Other Screw Fasteners. Machine screws are used with nuts, and washers, to join wood to metal or wood to many other materials, including wood. Machine screws come in different materials, just as do wood screws, and they may be used to produce an easily assembled and disassembled project. Among the popular holders for machine screws are T nuts, and brass screw inserts (Illus. 1.24 and 1.25).

A T nut is a type of nut that fits into a hole drilled in one wood surface. The T nut is set in place and then tapped down so that the teeth in the upper ring grip. The screw is then run into the T nut as if it were an ordinary nut, allowing assemblies to be mated. Ease of disassembly is built in.

Brass screw inserts work in a manner similar to a T nut as far as holding power goes, but it is inserted by screwing it into a hole drilled to size. An insert has coarse male threads on the outside, and finer female threads on the inside. The top of the brass insert is slotted to accept a standard flat-blade screwdriver tip of the appropriate size. The insert is turned down until the top is flush with its board, and then a machine screw, brass or steel, is driven into its internal threads. With insert fasteners, you can use knurled screws. Knurled screws are decorative and also offer easy disassembly, because no screwdriver is needed to install or remove them.

Other Threaded Fasteners. Lag screws—the proper term (but almost never used) is lag bolts, wood screw type—are heavier than common woods screws, and offer either a square or hexagonal head (Illus. 1.26). The coarser threads extend to a gimlet or cone point, with the threads covering slightly more than half of the screw length. A wrench is usually used to drive the lag screw, and the head should come to rest on a washer, not on wood. Lag screws serve where ordinary wood screws are too short or too light, and where driven spikes won't provide enough holding power.

Carriage bolts are intended for use in wood or metal, where the holes are drilled all the way through the pieces to be connected. There are three basic types of car-

Illus. 1.24 T nuts.

Illus. 1.25 Brass screw inserts.

Illus. 1.26 Lag screw in a flat bottom hole is driven using a deep socket wrench on its hexagonal head.

riage bolts, each type based on neck style: the square or common; the finned neck; and the ribbed neck (Illus. 1.27). Each style has a rounded over head above the neck. The necks on carriage bolts are intended, when used in wood, to be drawn up tight into the wood to prevent the head from turning. The shank fits through an exact-size hole. The bolt usually needs to be tapped through its holes with a hammer. The nut screws on with a washer used under the nut regardless of whether it covers wood, metal, or plastic.

Machine bolts may be used in place of carriage bolts in wood, **if** you have access to both sides of the work to run the thread and nut with wrenches (Illus. 1.28). Common flat washers are used under both the head and nut. Machine bolts generally have closer tolerances than do carriage bolts, for their primary use is for metal-to-metal joinery. The stove bolt is another related bolt that can be used in a similar manner to the carriage bolt or the machine bolt (Illus. 1.29 and 1.30). They can have a flat or rounded head and are slotted to accept a standard flat-blade screwdriver.

Nails. The nail is probably still the most useful mechanical fastener around as well as the easiest to use even if it is the least strong (Illus. 1.31). It certainly makes up for any lack of strength with its low cost and easy, fast installation.

Iron nails go back as far as the Roman occupation of what became Great Britain, and quite probably their use extends well

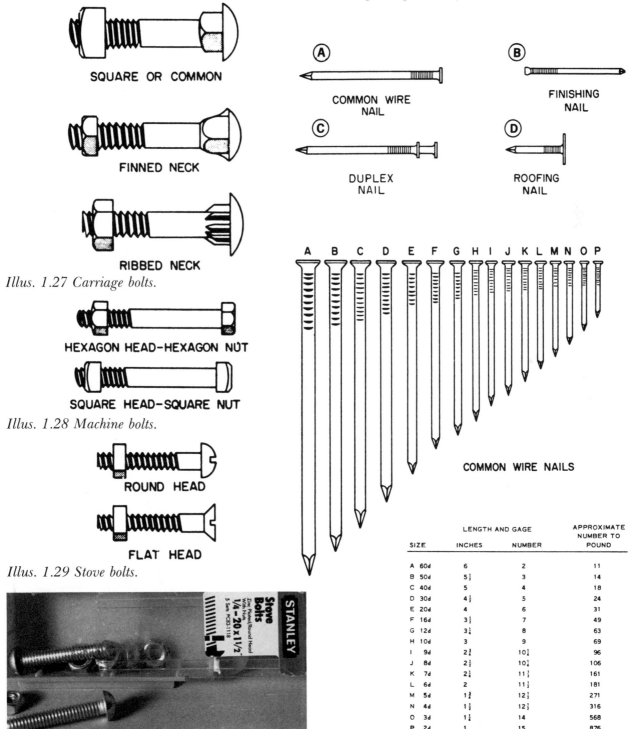

SQUARE OR COMMON

FINNED NECK

RIBBED NECK

Illus. 1.27 Carriage bolts.

HEXAGON HEAD–HEXAGON NUT

SQUARE HEAD–SQUARE NUT

Illus. 1.28 Machine bolts.

ROUND HEAD

FLAT HEAD

Illus. 1.29 Stove bolts.

Illus. 1.30 Stove bolts.

(A) COMMON WIRE NAIL

(B) FINISHING NAIL

(C) DUPLEX NAIL

(D) ROOFING NAIL

COMMON WIRE NAILS

| SIZE | LENGTH AND GAGE | | APPROXIMATE NUMBER TO POUND |
	INCHES	NUMBER	
A 60d	6	2	11
B 50d	5½	3	14
C 40d	5	4	18
D 30d	4½	5	24
E 20d	4	6	31
F 16d	3½	7	49
G 12d	3¼	8	63
H 10d	3	9	69
I 9d	2¾	10¼	96
J 8d	2½	10¼	106
K 7d	2¼	11½	161
L 6d	2	11½	181
M 5d	1¾	12½	271
N 4d	1½	12½	316
O 3d	1¼	14	568
P 2d	1	15	876

Illus. 1.31 Types of nails and nail sizes.

back from there. Roman nails were forged, which create differences in shape during their manufacture, but in general they were similar to today's wire nail.

Cut nails took over from forged nails in the late 1700s and early 1800s: early cut nails had handmade heads, but by about 1830 the entire nail was cut by machine.

Wire nails began as inexpensive substitutes for cut nails, but they were used only in the building of small boxes, not for general construction. By 1888, the size range grew to include 13 steps from 2d nails to 60d.

Nails are still sized by d, the abbreviation for penny, a method originally used by manufacturers to determine how many cents 100 nails—not a pound, but 100 nails—would cost.

Under 2d, or one inch, nails are classed as brads, and over 60d, or six inches, they're classed as spikes.

Common nails are used for general-purpose nailing from framing work on through some types of flooring installation. Shank styles differ: greater holding power is found with deformed shanks such as ring and screw. Coatings are available, and nails are often available hardened. Common nails also come in aluminum as well as galvanized, for outdoor uses.

Box nails are similar to common nails except that the head size relative to shank size differs slightly, with larger head sizes to shank diameters.

Post-and-truss nails are similar to common nails, but have a spiral or screw shank.

Wood-siding nails are special slim-shanked models designed to help prevent splitting of wood that must be nailed near edges or ends. It still makes sense to blunt the points and, within one inch of ends or edges, to drill pilot holes. Lengths run from two inches to three and one-half inches.

Finishing nails are slim, nearly headless, nails that come in sizes ranging from the one-inch brad finishing nail to at least 16d

Illus. 1.32 Finishing nails.

Illus. 1.33 Corrugated nails, and nailer.

(three and one-half inch) and typically beyond (Illus. 1.32). They come in clean mild steel, galvanized, and hot-dipped galvanized. Finishing nails are used because their small heads are easily set (with a nail set) below a board's surface, allowing a touch of putty to eliminate any nailed look.

One last nail-type fastener, corrugated nails, are extremely useful especially when working with plywood (Illus. 1.33). A special nailing device helps make their use easy and convenient.

Snap Fasteners. An important fastener when considering building a home for your pet is the snap-type clasp typically used for securing a pet's lead (Illus. 1.34). These snaps are available with several different kinds of locks and with or without swivels.

Illus. 1.34 Three kinds of Stanley snaps.

2
Tools for Projects and Some Useful Techniques

As far as possible, these pet-housing projects are designed for fairly common and easy-to-use tools, and to be built by most any small shop (Illus. 2.1). Many of these tools and some useful techniques will be described. There's little except for some turned items that cannot be completed with a circular saw (Illus. 2.2), a jigsaw (Illus. 2.3), and various hand tools (Illus. 2.4).

Illus. 2.1 Finger joints are most easily made on a table saw such as this, though they may also be cut with router jigs as well as by hand.

Illus. 2.3 A jigsaw: this maker calls this a bayonet saw. By either name, they are great for cutting curves and curved bevels in stock that is moderately thick.

Illus. 2.2 This is a good example of a lightweight, easy-to-handle but heavy-duty circular saw.

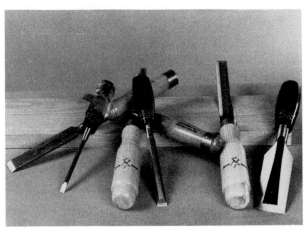

Illus. 2.4 Several types of top-grade chisels are always useful.

Much will be easier with a band saw (Illus. 2.5), a table saw (Illus. 2.6), and a radial-arm saw (Illus. 2.7). Other similar tools (Illus. 2.8) and accessories, some of which will be described, may also be helpful. Certain trim pieces will be easier with a scroll saw (Illus. 2.9) and a router (Illus. 2.10, 2.11), but most may also be cut with a jigsaw, or a hand scroll saw. Fancy tools aren't essential, only handy—and nice to have.

Illus. 2.8 The ease and smoothness of a sprayed-on finish is only a part of the usefulness of an air compressor: more and more tools are being made for use with a compressor as the main power source.

*Illus. 2.5 Band saws allow you to cut odd shapes and curves with ease, and with **no danger** of kickback.*

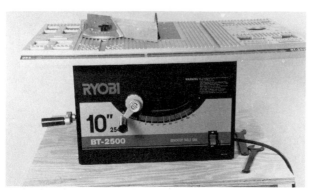

Illus. 2.6 Powerful, yet portable, this small saw is also accurate.

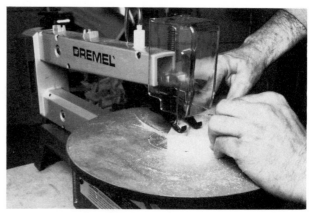

Illus. 2.9 This two-speed scroll saw is, of the low cost models the writer has tried, the superior model.

Illus. 2.7 This small radial-arm saw works well; the arm carries easily.

Illus. 2.10 Heavy-duty plunge routers drive large bits and are also good for production work, but they tend to be tiring to use.

Illus. 2.11 This D-handled router is a classic, and it is easier to handle than the huge routers; as well, it is quite powerful (at one and one-half horsepower).

Illus. 2.12 These tools are helpful in measuring and applying measurements; the stick on the upper left is a Lufkin glass-cutting guide and is exceptionally handy when clamped as a saw or router straightedge guide.

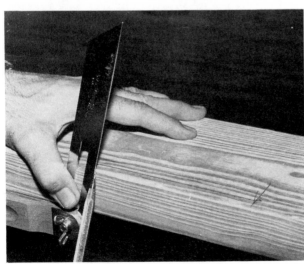

Illus. 2.13 A sliding T-bevel is one of the most useful layout tools.

Measuring Tools

The basics of any woodworking project are the tools with which you transfer measurements from plans to wood (Illus. 2.12) as well as the solidity of the construction. Too, the ease of construction will usually depend on how accurately those measurements are transferred (Illus. 2.13).

Measurements are both taken and provided with several tools, among which are folding rules and measuring tapes. For tighter spots, and greater accuracy, there are also calipers (Illus. 2.14)—many calipers also have rod-style depth gauges, which are a great help when making inside measurements of some joints (mortises, dowel hole depths, etc.).

Measuring tapes come in a great many lengths and in a number of widths (Illus. 2.15). For most project purposes, lengths above a dozen feet aren't necessary, though they may be handy for siting various doghouses or similar items. When buying a measuring tape, go for the absolute best you can afford, with the widest possible tape. The wider the tape, the stiffer it is, thus the longer it lasts (and the easier it is to read).

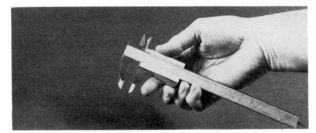

Illus. 2.14 Calipers provide a high degree of accuracy in both metric and English measurements, and they are often equipped with a depth rod.

Illus. 2.15 Tilt the tape to get the markings closer to the piece being marked, thus making sure any deviation is small.

Folding rules usually come in six-foot and eight-foot lengths (Illus. 2.16). The good ones have brass hardware, and some models offer a sliding extension that also serves to help take depth measurements.

The basics of measuring are quite straightforward, only requiring the addition of a simple technique such as tilting the tape or rule when a mark is being made on the workpiece. Such a tilt assures that the appropriate mark is close to the surface rather than as much as one-eighth of an inch in the air, on a curl of the tape or thickness of the rule. Accuracy is increased slightly, which is always a help.

Marks may be made with standard pencils, carpenter's pencils or scribes (Illus. 2.17). While a scribe is the most precise marker, the thick lead of a carpenter's pencil properly used can be nearly as precise, and the mark is more easily seen. Simply cut the pencil down with a knife to form a

wedge shape, and then sand the point sharp—I take a shortcut and use a power-sander to do the entire job.

Other measuring and marking tools abound, but the most critical ones for woodworking projects are squares.

Squares. For small- to moderate-sized woodworking projects, these include the sliding T-bevel, the basic try square, the combination square, and the framing square (Illus. 2.18). All come in variations, both in size and type, so there is almost always a proper square for any job.

Try squares offer a basic, and solid, 90° setting, often with a not-so precise, short 45° along the handle facing the blade. The try square tends to be the most precise, because the handle and blade are solidly held together.

Combination squares offer versatility in an attempt to be most things for most people. They do succeed reasonably well as adjustable squares, both for 90° and 45°, and as markers. As a level, the combination square fails—that bubble takes too much of a beating to retain accuracy for long. The try square is more accurate than the combination square when used at 90°, but it is not as convenient. Setting the combination square blade at a specific distance allows use of the scribe that is often included in the handle to mark that distance on a board.

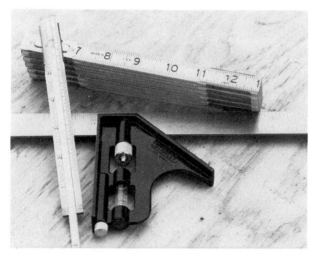

Illus. 2.16 Folding rule and combination square.

Illus. 2.17 Combination square and scribe.

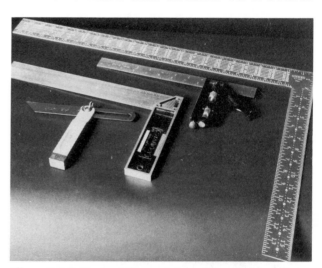

Illus. 2.18 From left to right: sliding T-bevel, try square, combination square (with scribe in handle), and framing square.

Framing squares offer many features in a larger (standard size is 24 inches by 16 inches) format.

Work quality depends both on the squares themselves and on how well they're used: the basic shop needs at least one good combination square and one good try square. Any other squares are always a useful and welcomed addition to any shop (Illus. 2.19).

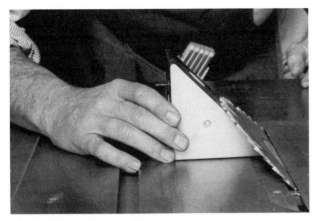

Illus. 2.19 Krypton-bulbed square for saws (and other tools) gives remarkable precision of setup.

Illus. 2.20 Tenon saw or backsaw.

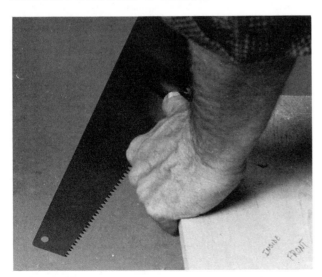

Illus. 2.21 Starting a cut with Sandvik's hard-toothed saw. Note tooth pattern, which differs greatly from the standard pattern of crosscut handsaws.

Handsaws

Saws are the primary cutting tools for woodworking (Illus. 2.20). For these pet-home projects, nothing fancy in the saw line is needed: a ten-points-per-inch panel saw; a 12 inch or larger backsaw; a coping, or scroll, saw. If you use metal, or harder plastics, you might want to use a hacksaw. For rougher cuts, one of the newer hard-toothed saws, with eight points per inch, works well, cutting quickly and neatly. These are the only low-cost handsaws I've ever seen that are worth what they cost (Illus. 2.21, 2.22).

A mitre box is also handy. There are a number of versions, but a style I recommend is a full-degree-adjustable design with its own saw that has a changeable blade (and blades for both metal and wood) (Illus. 2.23).

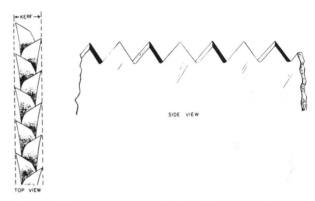

Illus. 2.22 Standard crosscut handsaw tooth pattern.

Illus. 2.23 Nobex mitre box has changeable blades, so it may also be used with soft metals such as copper, aluminum, and brass.

Proper use is needed with any handsaw: start a cut to the waste side of the cut line, guiding with the thumb knuckle against the side of the blade until the teeth bite. Cut with the handle at a comfortable angle, generally between 45° and 60°.

Saw care is simple (Illus. 2.24). Make sure the blade won't strike the ground, or other objects, under the wood being cut. Make sure there are no nails in the wood being cut. Do not force a saw that kinks in a cut; back out, clean the blade, and try again. Often, the saw kinks because it is the board that is twisting. Whenever possible, handsaws should be hung up, rather than being laid down. Keep the blade lightly oiled, free of gum or pitch build-up.

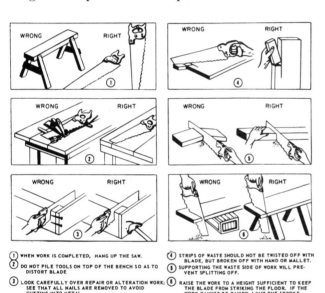

Illus. 2.24 Care and use of saws.

Illus. 2.25 Both straight-claw hammers have fibreglass handles, while the right-hand curved-claw hammer has a tubular metal handle.

Fastening Tools

Hammers, screwdrivers, and staplers are the basic wood fastening tools.

Hammers are available in many styles and sizes, but for pet-housing projects, a good quality 16-ounce, curved-claw hammer is suitable. Balance with curved claws is a bit better than with ripping claws, and a 16-ounce head offers a good choice between lightweight and heavyweight (head weights vary from 13 ounces to 28 ounces). While I prefer the fibreglass handle, I often use tubular metal and wood, as well (Illus. 2.25).

Screwdrivers come in all the expected head styles, to fit old and new screw-head patterns. Select for head style, and for quality. A good screwdriver is one with a handle that fits your hand well, and with a strong blade of an alloy that lasts. Tip machining should be clean and neat. The best-handling screwdrivers are those, available from several manufacturers, with wedge-shaped handles that spread out as they reach the shank of the screwdriver.

Whenever you use a screwdriver, it is a good idea first to prepare pilot holes (Illus. 2.26). The hand drill is the simplest way to quickly produce pilot holes.

Staplers are useful for attaching fabrics to wood as well as light woods to heavier woods. Since I have been using air-powered staplers, I no longer find myself using hand or electric staplers, except for hammer style staplers (Illus. 2.27). Air-powered staplers are simpler, and they seem more efficient and less likely to jam than electric versions. As well, air compressors have improved, requiring less care (Illus. 2.28).

Illus. 2.26 A top-of-the-line hand drill from Stanley.

Power Tools

The list of power tools always starts with electric drills: everyone either has one, or should have one.

Electric drills. It is no longer necessary to be linked to an outlet to use an electric drill: cordless drills have come into their own, offering good power, and superb convenience (Illus. 2.29). Some models are extremely powerful while requiring only 12 volts of battery storage power yet also offering a quick charge feature (Illus. 2.30 and 2.31). I consider those shown in Illus. 2.30 and 2.31 to be the top of the list of the very good cordless drills. Such top-grade

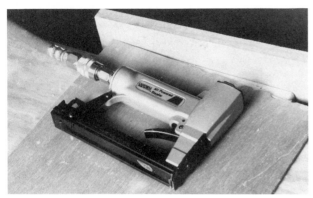

Illus. 2.27 An air-powered stapler from Campbell-Hausfeld.

Illus. 2.28 Newer oilless compressors need far less care than do oiled types.

Illus. 2.29 New cordless drills have ample power for bits such as these brad point styles.

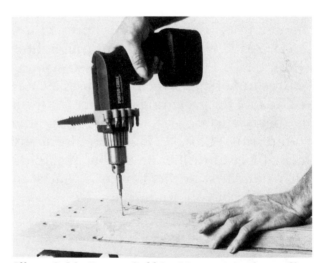

Illus. 2.30 Porter-Cable's Magnaquench cordless drill with Vermont-American's bandoleer of tips.

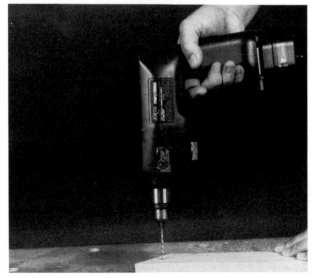

Illus. 2.31 Faster pilot holes come with the Skil Top Gun and its second, high-speed range.

cordless drills are often sold with an extra battery pack included, which makes keeping going all day even simpler (Illus. 2.32).

Standard electric drills also come in many versions and chucks sizes. Select for durability as well as for power. The drill is one tool where buying cheap doesn't pay, because the very low-cost models don't offer many features and have a short life. For most purposes, a three-eighths-inch chuck electric drill with a variable-speed and reversible motor that draws over 3.5 amperes will work well.

There are a great many useful types of drill bit available. Forstner-type bits require a slow-speed, powerful drill, but make nicely machined, flat-bottomed holes (Illus. 2.33). Some Forstner-type drills are large enough to be useful with a drill press (Illus. 2.34). Spade bits cut a fast, but rough, hole (Illus. 2.35). There are some low-cost alternatives to Forstner-type bits (Illus. 2.36). A useful tool for preparing a surface for flush or below-surface screw-fastening is the countersink (Illus. 2.37). There are many other types of drill bits available, including such standards as the Vermont American brad point bits shown in Illus. 2.29.

Illus. 2.34 Large Disston Forstner drills.

Illus. 2.35 Spade bits.

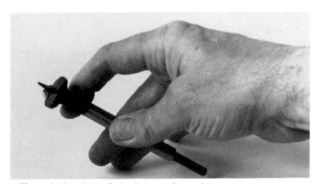

Illus. 2.36 Stanley's Powerbore bit.

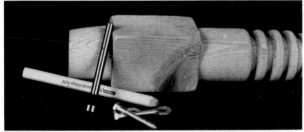

Illus. 2.32 The Black & Decker Professional cordless drill offers good power, great durability.

Illus. 2.33 Forstner-type bit leaning against the turned leg requires slow speeds, a powerful drill, but it makes flat-bottomed, nicely machined holes.

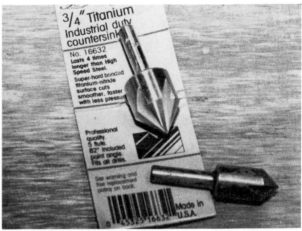

Illus. 2.37 Countersinks come in a great many styles and sizes.

Power saws provide great versatility in cutting, with the all-around most useful being the table saw, a tool that is as versatile as the router (Illus. 2.38).

Table saws come in a wide range of types, sizes, and styles, with some light enough to be moved easily from one job site to another. Others are not easily moved at all: my main table saw does not move (Illus. 2.39). The unit weighs upwards of 750 pounds, and is not meant to be portable. The basic saw weighs over 400 pounds, while the rip fence and sliding table add the rest of the weight. The increase in usefulness of the tool with those two accessories is considerable.

Selecting a table saw is not a simple task because of the wide variety on the market. The blade sizes available may range from four inches up to 14 inches, while power can vary from fractional horsepower to three-phase multihorsepower. It is a rare small shop, however, that requires three-phase electrical power; that is primarily for industrial needs and is found mostly in five horsepower and up tools.

Probably of greater importance, once a basic one to three horsepower motor is decided on, is the quality of the saw itself. Tolerances need to be tight, the table precisely machined, and the various adjusters well made. The mitre slots must be precise, and the rip fence well made. Both the mitre gauge and the rip fence may be replaced with accessories such as the Excalibur units, but remember that such units alone cost hundreds of dollars (Illus. 2.40). They expand the capabilities of most table saws, but they also eliminate portability (my Excalibur fence and sliding table—neither of them the largest models available—make my saw something over 8½-feet wide, as well as heavy).

Illus. 2.39 The Delta Unisaw, with the Excalibur rip fence, is an excellent machine, both powerful and accurate, but it can't even remotely be thought of as portable.

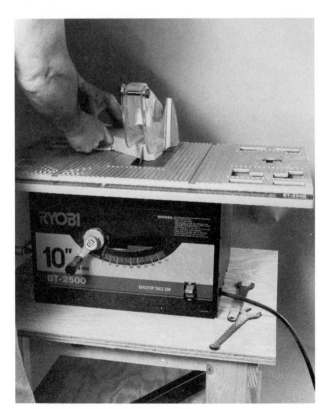

Illus. 2.38 One table saw that is particularly lightweight, and easily portable.

Illus. 2.40 Maple board being crosscut using the Mule sliding table.

Finger Joints with the Table Saw. The finger joint, or box joint, widely used in mass-produced products at the turn of the nineteenth century, is still a winner in most applications for which the dovetail used to be considered best: it supplies a huge gluing surface (Illus. 2.41 and 2.42). Finger, or box, joints may be dowelled through the pins with a single dowel (or a double dowel on really large sizes), after which it will resist extensional forces, with or without gluing. With a single dowel used as a pivot, and the ends of the fingers rounded a bit, the joint becomes a hinge.

Finger joints are so well suited to table saws to be a specialty. There are several jig styles that work well, one of which is the commercial Accu-Joint jig (Illus. 2.43). There are really only two objections: the tiny locating pins are exceptionally easy to lose; the jig itself is only a foot wide, limiting the width of any panels being jointed.

Most of the time, that limit is not serious, because 90 percent of the joints for drawers and small boxes are cut in stock much narrower than one foot (Illus. 2.44). With the width limit, however, comes the ability to easily and quickly cut finger joints in three sizes: ¼-inch, ⅜-inch, and ½-inch joints are all readily made by laying a specific template over the basic template and changing the dado blade width.

Making your own finger-joint jig is far from difficult, requiring only a few bits of wood, some accuracy, and a dado blade set. A dado blade set is a good accessory to have as it is required for the Accu-Joint jig and a great deal of other table-saw work.

A shop-made jig means a separate jig for each joint size—a different size cutout for each size of finger joint. At the same time, you are not limited to any restricted number of joint sizes. If you need one-inch finger joints, a jig can be made to produce

Illus. 2.41 Note the huge glue area of finger joints.

Illus. 2.43 The Accu-Joint jig is being used to make large finger joints in cherry.

Illus. 2.42 Finger-jointed oak is to be used to make the apron for a tool table. Note the slight extra length of the pins, for easy cleanup with just a fast sanding.

Illus. 2.44 Finger-jointed maple and walnut. A groove has been cut to accommodate the bottom for the Cat Resting Box project.

them—though most dada heads will require two passes per joint cutout with such wide pins. The maximum cut with many dado heads is $^{13}/_{16}$ of an inch, which readily allows single-pass finger joints up to $^{3}/_{4}$-inches wide. Most of the time, more modest finger joints provide a better appearance, with $^{1}/_{2}$ inch being the largest pin size used with wood up to about $1^{1}/_{2}$-inch thickness. The thinner the stock, the narrower the pin that will provide a top-grade appearance finger joint.

The simplest jig possible is best (Illus. 2.45). Start with a mitre gauge extension that will pass the blade, or dado head, on the side you prefer to work. Measuring care is imperative with any jig. Any sloppiness in jig measurement or assembly will mean that joints will not fit. Start with a piece of oak, maple, ash, or similar hardwood for the greatest durability and accuracy. Soft woods may be used, but are not as sturdy and do not retain their accuracy as long. The extension should be at least three-inches high and 16-inches wide, with both height and width increasing as the size of boards to be joined increases. The extension is securely screwed to the mitre gauge, and set to allow the mitre gauge free movement in its slot.

Set a $^{3}/_{8}$-inch dado blade to cut $^{3}/_{4}$-inches deep, and check the dimensions first by measuring, then by making a practice cut in scrap stock. This jig is meant to last for years, so you must be sure it is accurate. When the setting is exactly right, make a pass with the actual piece. Measure over $^{3}/_{8}$ of an inch from the first slot and cut a second $^{3}/_{8}$-inch by $^{3}/_{4}$-inch slot.

Into the first slot, insert a $^{3}/_{4}$-inch by $^{3}/_{8}$-inch by $2^{1}/_{2}$-inch stop block. Then, secure the entire jig to the mitre gauge, making sure that the second, or open, jig slot is directly over the set dado blade. Vary the size of slot and finger to suit the size of joints needed.

Make a guide strip the width of the dado-blade cut, and use that to offset the board being cut. Place the guide strip alongside the board edge, both held upright and butted against the stop block (spring clamps work well here). Make the first pass over the dado blade to give an L-shaped cut on the board. Remove the guide strip, move the board over so that the L-shaped cut fits over the stop block, and place the mating piece in front of the already cut piece, its edge butted against the stop block. Clamp lightly, and pass over the dado blade. Move

Finger-Joint Jig

Vary slot and finger size according to joint size needed. Mount to mitre jig so that the jig works from the side of the table you are used to using. This mount works to the right side of the blade.

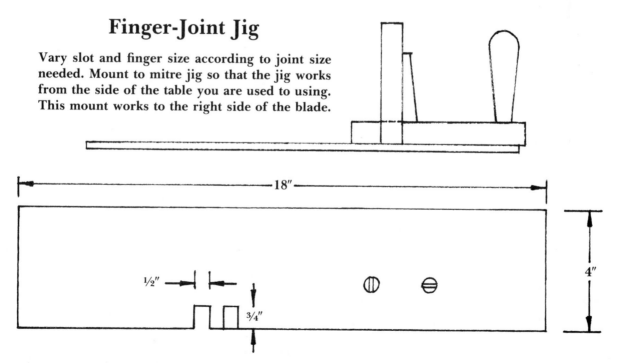

18"

4"

$^{1}/_{2}$"

$^{3}/_{4}$"

Illus. 2.45 Finger-joint jig plan.

the entire assembly over to the just-cut notch (the notch moves onto the stop block), and repeat the cut. Continue until the entire width is cut. The pieces will mate properly, and you will have cut the edges of two sides at one time, a solid time-saver over most such jigs.

For each joint size, you will need to make a separate jig. The possible sizes are nearly infinite, but the four most popular are ¼ inch, ⅜ inch, ½ inch, and ⅝ inch. When you want to make a jig of a different size, replace the ⅜-inch specification on the jig design with the desired size. For the ½-inch and ⅝-inch sizes, it is practical to increase the pin length (the ¾-inch measurement) to one inch.

For ease of fit, add about ⅟₃₂ of an inch to the cut depth for the sockets. This allows the pins to extend just far enough so that some light sanding will finish the finger joint (Illus. 2.46). If the depth is too shallow, the only way to finish the joint is to sand the entire side.

Grooves and Dadoes on the Table Saw. Grooves and dadoes differ in only one way: grooves are made with the grain of the wood (Illus. 2.47), while dadoes are cut against, or across, the grain of the wood. Admittedly, this distinction becomes obscure when the wood being cut is plywood (Illus. 2.48). When there is no discernible grain direction, it is common practice to refer to a cut in the face of a board as a dado and as a groove when it is cut on an edge. Dado sets are simple accessories, being stacked blade assemblies that give a wider kerf, or cut (Illus. 2.49). The outer blades are similar to standard saw blades, while the inner—or chipper—blades commonly have only two teeth on opposite sides of the blade. The chipper blades clean out the area between the outer blades, producing a set-width groove, or dado.

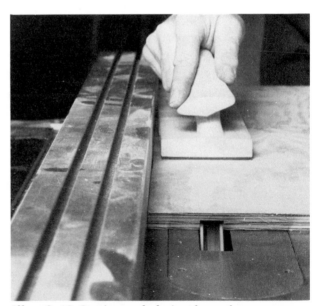

Illus. 2.48 Cutting a dado in plywood.

Illus. 2.46 Sanding off the extra pin length on a finger joint.

Illus. 2.47 Groove cut in from edge of pine board.

Illus. 2.49 Stacked dado set.

Other dado blades exist such as the single-blade or dual-blade "wobbler" units. The one or two blades are set to wobble at a maximum specified distance, producing a cut of the same size as the wobble. Such dado blades tend to leave more material in the bottoms of the grooves than do standard chipper sets, but they also tend to be faster and easier to set up.

Dado blades are useful for other types of cuts. The rabbet cut is one. A rabbet is an L-shaped recess cut into the wood, into which another piece of wood (or other material) fits to produce a rabbet joint. The rabbet cut is set up along the rip fence, leaving no lip on the cut. I prefer to work with an auxiliary fence for rabbets, reducing the chance of pinging my aluminum fence with the carbide tip of the dado blade. To make an auxiliary fence, use a straight piece of wood and attach it with screws through the factory holes in the metal fence (if there are no holes, drill two). Get the auxiliary fence down on the table, but not so tight that the metal fence won't move with it in place. Now, cut a relief arch or pocket in the fence facing to allow the waste to move away from the blade. This arch will need to be a different depth for different cuts; so start with the blade lowered and make a slight cut in at about two-thirds the depth of the facing width (if you used a ¾-inch thick board, cut in about ½ inch). Raise the blade slowly to increase the height of the relief arch, to a maximum of ¾ of an inch to one inch.

To use the dado setup to cut a rabbet, set the depth of the blades to the necessary point after installing the blades to give a width about ¹⁄₁₆ to ⅛ of an inch more than the width required for the actual rabbet. Set the auxiliary fence so that it produces the required width, and lock all the settings. Feed the material through keeping a snug fit against the fence facing. Use push tools for any cut where the blade is going blind, the case with all rabbets and dadoes.

To use the dado setup for egg-crate style finger joints, make sure the notch is the exact width of the stock thickness used, and the depth of cut exactly half the height of the stock used. You may, for square projects, mark a single piece of wood and clamp the other sides together, thus cutting the entire project as a single unit.

Lap Joints on the Table Saw. Lap joints—and in particular, half-laps—are rapidly made by notching, using a dado setup to cut away stock. This method is particularly valuable for lap joints that are not at board ends but in the middle, where a standard blade would take too long to make all the passes needed to clear the notch for the lap. The dado setup is used to set the end markings or sides of the notch, cutting first at one end, and then at the other. After that, multiple passes clear the middle of the notch, and the process can be repeated if boards are to be cross lapped.

End laps work in much the same manner, but only the inward side of the area to be cleared is cut first, with multiple passes made until the end of the board is reached.

Laps may be mitred, angled, and dovetailed, as well as made to match boards of different thicknesses besides being cut as usual to half depth for two boards of equal thickness.

Mitre and Butt Joints by Power Saw. The mitre joint is a variant of the butt joint in that pieces cut, usually at 45° angles, are butted together and fastened in place (Illus. 2.50). Typically a mitre is used to join boards at a right angle, but it can be used to

Illus. 2.50 Perfect Miter (TM) eases mitre setup on table saws, and eliminates any need to use the mitre gauge.

join at any angle. The mitre cut is always one-half of the desired angle (Illus. 2.51). The special feature of the mitre is that it hides the end grain (Illus. 2.52). It is useful for picture frames, door and window moulding, and similar objects. Mitre joints are also used when working with plywood because they leave only the surface of the plywood showing, not the underlying plies. Thus,

Illus. 2.51 Cutting the opposite side.

Illus. 2.52 The result is a right-angle mitre joint that hides the end grain.

Illus. 2.53 Edge mitres are a version of a bevel; when cut along the grain of the board, they are sometimes called rip mitres.

the mitre joint is a cabinetry joint for both mouldings and frame carcass construction (Illus. 2.53).

The table saw is not the absolutely perfect tool for creating smooth crosscuts: the radial-arm saw is better at this particular job, but is limited in crosscut capacity (Illus. 2.54). My DeWalt 12-inch radial-arm saw, for example, is large for a home shop saw, but has a crosscut capacity, in ¾-inch material, of only 16 inches, and somewhat less in thicker material. To get really decent crosscuts, it's necessary to go to industrial performance radial-arm saws, such as Delta's 18-inch model, but you may find these too expensive. Even then, the crosscut capacity is 23¼ inches, just about what you'll need to slice across a kitchen countertop. If you need to mitre that countertop, you're out of luck (the capacity is 19 inches left, 11 inches right). Even my little Ryobi folding radial-arm saw offers a decent crosscut—¹⁄₁₆ inch short of 11 inches—but not a great one. The smaller saw, however, is priced about one-quarter the larger home shop saw; there is tremendous value for the somewhat smaller cut on a comparison of capacity versus cost.

For most common widths of crosscuts, the radial-arm saw tends to be superior to the table saw (Illus. 2.55). The exception is if you manage to come up with one of the

Illus. 2.54 Power mitre boxes also do a fine job of producing mitres in fairly thick, somewhat narrow, stock.

versions of sliding tables now made for table saws (Illus. 2.56). You might also make a mitre box yourself, easing the chore of getting accurate mitres (Illus. 2.57).

Use hardwood only, maple or oak, for the mitre slot guide, cut to fit your saw's mitre gauge slot. Make the guide the appropriate length, at least two feet, and size—most mitre gauge slots are ⅜ inch by ¾ inch.

Cut the base of your jig depending on the size of your table saw. The plan calls for a jig base 24 inches deep (parallel with the saw blade) and 18 inches wide, a reasonable minimum size (Illus. 2.57). If the table is any larger than this, then wider is usually better than longer. Fir, birch, oak, or any good ¾-inch plywood will work well. For extra durability, a laminate can be added on the upper surface to suit any size or style. For a slightly less expensive jig base, the waste piece from cutting out the opening for a sink in a laminated plywood countertop can be used. However, it is best to turn this kind of laminate down when used for the jig base.

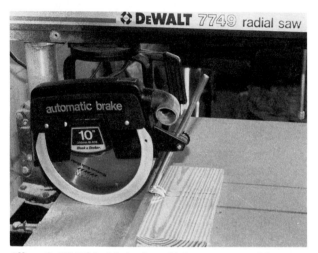

Illus. 2.55 This 10-inch radial-arm saw, with a top-grade blade, gives smooth crosscuts, bevels, and mitres.

Illus. 2.56 Setting up for repetitive cuts on the table saw using a Mule sliding table with a stop.

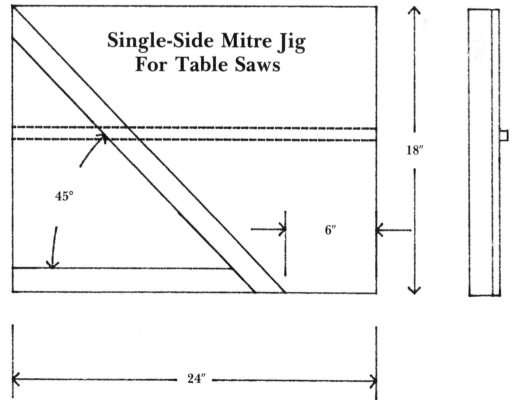

Illus. 2.57 Single side mitre jig plan.

Lower the saw blade all the way, and place the hardwood guide piece in the slot, even with the front of the table. Make sure that the fit is proper, allowing the guide to slide readily without being loose. Coat the top of the hardwood slot guide with glue, and clamp your jig base in place even with the front of your saw table.

Allow the glue to set. Drill and countersink three holes along the guide strip—two inches from each end and one hole in the middle. Place the screws. Once the guide is attached, square to the base, slide the jig back and raise the saw blade. Make a partial cut through the jig base along the long dimension—straight on into the blade, at a 90° angle to the front.

Use the inner edge of this saw cut to mark two lines; one continuing along parallel to the cut, and a second at a 45° angle as shown in the plan (Illus. 2.57). This jig may be made with a 60° angle, or, for that matter, a 22½° angle. I suggest making one jig for each, thus suiting most standard mitre cuts.

Make the angle bars from two-by-four stock, planed down to give sharp edges and a wide dimension of about three inches. Place the pieces along the two marked lines to fit them properly, but attach them one at a time with glue and screws. Repeat and continue the straight cut along the long side of the jig to trim the mitre bar angle piece to a flush 45°.

To complete your jig, glue fine grit sandpaper to the face of the 45° mitre bar angle piece so that material being cut can't slip as easily. If you wish, you can also add a straightedge and a handle. An oversized Shaker peg makes a good handle.

Butt joints are probably the simplest as well as the most common joints used for woodwork. They are readily produced, both cross and along the grain, on a table saw. A simple crosscut guide that you can easily make can assist in getting accurate crosscuts on your table saw (Illus. 2.58). Rip cuts are truly the table saw's forte. The table saw can produce long butt joints quite

Crosscut Guide

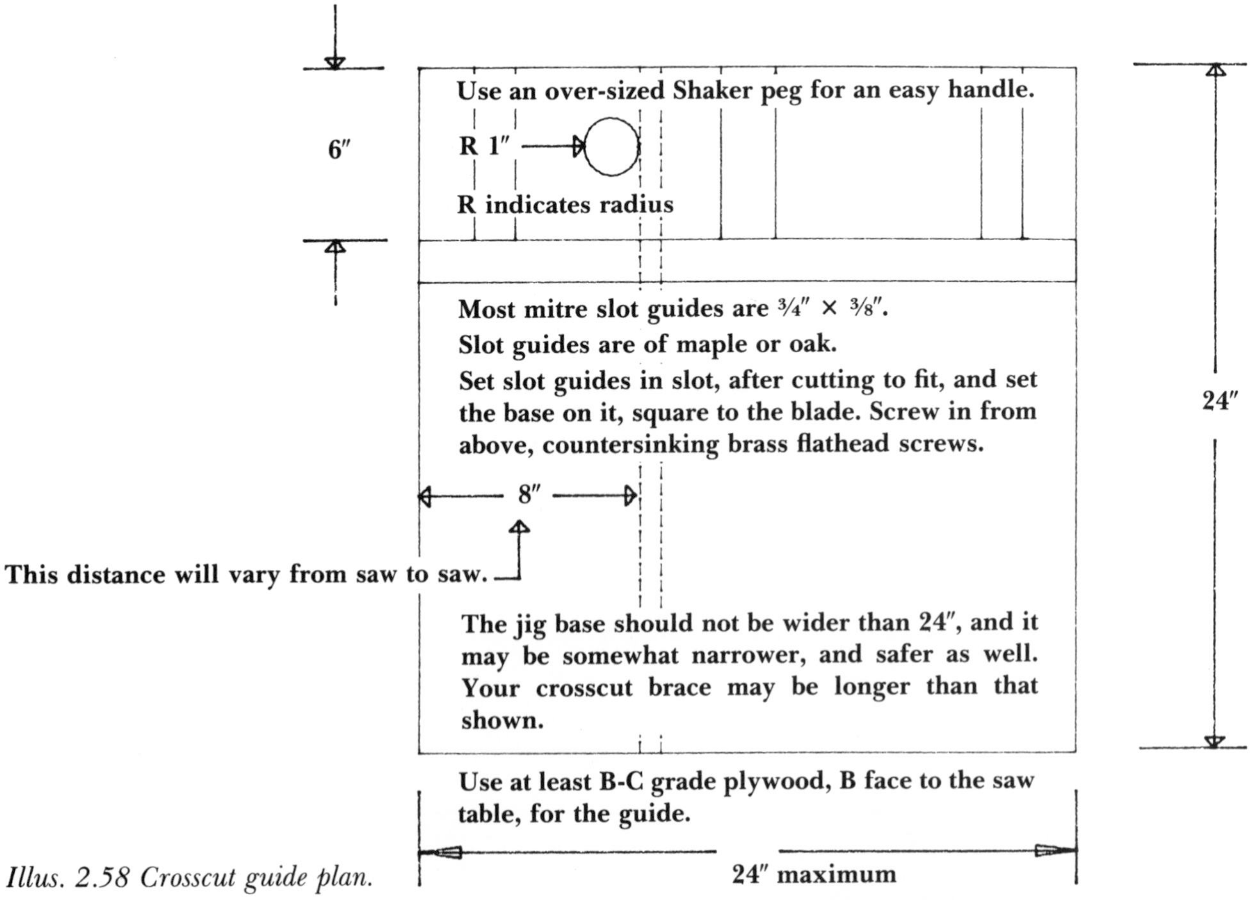

6″

Use an over-sized Shaker peg for an easy handle.

R 1″ →

R indicates radius

Most mitre slot guides are ¾″ × ⅜″.
Slot guides are of maple or oak.
Set slot guides in slot, after cutting to fit, and set the base on it, square to the blade. Screw in from above, countersinking brass flathead screws.

8″

This distance will vary from saw to saw.

The jig base should not be wider than 24″, and it may be somewhat narrower, and safer as well. Your crosscut brace may be longer than that shown.

24″

Use at least B-C grade plywood, B face to the saw table, for the guide.

24″ maximum

Illus. 2.58 Crosscut guide plan.

well. A decent set of hold-downs and feather boards help to maintain cut evenness (Illus. 2.59), while a top-quality rip blade provides a good glue line (Illus. 2.60).

Be sure to use a rip blade, in particular, for long rip cuts. Combination blades are fine for shorter rip cuts as well as cutoff (across the grain) work, but they are not suitable for extensive rips in quality hardwoods. Feed fairly fast according to wood thickness. Feed will have to slow way down on underpowered saws and with truly heavy woods such as oaks or maple, but generally, it is best to rip as fast as the saw will safely accept the wood.

In order to feed rapidly, you need a good rip blade—my preference runs to a blade with 24 teeth—numbers of teeth are for a 10-inch blade (Illus. 2.60)—that is carbide-tipped, with an alternate top bevel grind, and a hook of about 20°. This description is similar to many combination blades, except for the hook angle. Crosscut blades have much less of a hook angle, often as little as 7°, while combination blades have about double that number of degrees. Whatever the hook angle, be sure to use an alternate top bevel grind blade, though. For rougher work, a blade with 18 teeth and a flat top grind works well.

Band Saws. Other power saws are available, but they are less accurate than the table saw, giving a rougher joint. The main advantage is that they allow more speed in construction. There is one other stationary saw, in particular, the band saw, that will do almost everything the table saw will do with little or no danger of kickback. Kickback is the prime drawback of table saws, and unfortunately, it is a function of blade design and rotation that cannot be totally eliminated. The band saw also offers great ease on jobs the table saw cannot do at all well such as cutting curves.

Band saws differ from table saws in that the blade does not spin, but rotates around two—or in some models three—wheels and passes through a set of guides held above the work and table. The blade is endless, a welded loop (Illus. 2.61). It may vary in width from ⅛ of an inch to as much as 3 inches on band saws aimed at resawing operations—resawing is the procedure of ripping a board through its tallest dimension, to get two thinner boards.

Illus. 2.59 Hold-downs help keep rip cuts straight.

Illus. 2.60 Top-grade rip blades are essential to good cuts.

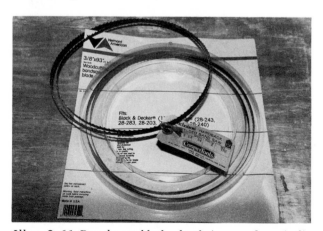

Illus. 2.61 Band-saw blades by their very form indicate the difference in saw operation between the band saw and the table saw.

Circular Saws and Their Use. Circular saws are primarily used in general construction work to cut mitre and butt joints. Their accuracy depends on the user's experience as well as on jigs used to assist in the cut. Accuracy also depends on the quality of the saw itself and on its blade and the blade sharpness (Illus. 2.62).

In most instances, a carbide-tipped blade is best (Illus. 2.63), but when you are cutting old wood—wood that might have nails embedded—use a standard steel blade designed for cutting flooring. Nails when struck sometimes dislodge carbide tips and send them flying—an experience far better read about than learned in person. A combination blade for general use reduces the need for either changing blades when making both rip and crosscuts or using two saws. You could also use a rip or cut off blade. To assure extra smooth cuts of either type, al-ways use the appropriate blade. For the best mitres, use a top-grade planer combination blade. Also be sure to use the proper tool for the particular job and kind of cuts required (Illus. 2.64, 2.65, 2.66).

Illus. 2.64 For bevel cuts, a radial-arm saw can be just right.

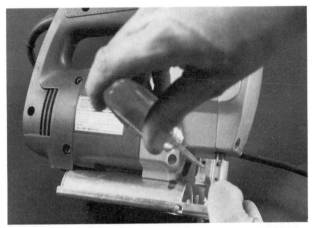

Illus. 2.65 Jigsaws are versatile, and changing blades is a simple operation.

Illus. 2.62 Circular saw with layout in plywood leaving an allowance for the kerf. Check a kerf to see, but usually ⅛ inch is fine.

Illus. 2.63 Both blades have carbide tips and aggressive tooth patterns, but the blade on the right is for rips and rough work.

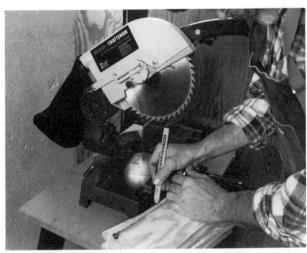

Illus. 2.66 A compound mitre saw such as this offers an alternative to the radial-arm saw that is powerful and heavily made.

The rip guide, a feature often ignored on circular saws, provides an excellent guide for long rips. It adjusts to allow the appropriate cutoff of material with the grain, but the guide is not useful for cross-grain cuts. The guide is easy to use; the shaft slides into the slots on the saw's base, and the screw (or screws) is tightened once the distance is set. Use the guide on the outside edge of the work and make the cut.

For deeper rip cuts, and for crosscuts, a guide board jig is needed. Go to a lumberyard and have a piece of tempered hardboard (¼-inch thick) cut about a foot wide and five-to-ten feet long (depending on the lengths of the cuts you expect to need). You may want to make several of these guides in different lengths. To that tempered hardboard, glue and screw a ½-inch thick by 4-inch wide board that is as straight as possible. Fasten along the long side, keeping the thicker board even with one long edge of the thin board.

The last step in preparing the jig is simple. Measure the width of your saw base plate to the blade, and set the jig in place. Clamp it on the material to be cut. Cut both the jig and the material. After this, you can measure the material, and place the jig so that the cut off edge is at the edge of where the cut will be—assuming you always use the same circular saw with this jig (mark both the jig and the saw, if you have more than one circular saw, so that they can be paired for proper use).

Woodworking with a Router. Routers are one of the most useful woodworking tools. If you do not have a router, but plan to continue woodworking, I recommend that you buy one. Select a model with at least one horsepower, preferably with a ½-inch collet—though a ¼-inch collet will do if that's what the bit is. The smaller collet chuck diameter makes for less accurate machining. A plunge router may be handy, but is far from essential. Many of the best routers do not offer a plunge feature. Under heavy use, plunge routers wear out somewhat sooner, but this is not a problem for nonproduction work if the router is of good quality.

Routers on the market today offer more features and power than ever before. Power ranges from one-half horsepower to five horsepower. For most home workshop uses, a quality router offering one or more horsepower will serve for years. Lighter duty routers are too limited for some work, while the very heavy duty models—those of three horsepower and up—are heavier and harder to handle, though they can really turn out work.

Safety is important: there is no guard on the bit. The bit will be turning from 15,000 to 20,000 rpms, so once it is removed from the wood, or if it recoils from the wood, there is danger. Always change bits or work on the bit only when the router is unplugged. Let the bit reach full speed before plunging or otherwise entering the work. Always let the bit stop on or in the work before lifting the router.

Router Dovetail Systems. There are several router dovetail jig systems available including the Keller system, the Leigh dovetail jig, and systems marketed by Sears. I will describe the Keller system with which I have had very good results. The Keller dovetail jig units make basic through dovetails, with fixed pin spacings, in three sizes. The templates come in pairs. One of the pair makes tails; the other produces pins. Keller includes dovetail bits of appropriate size and style with each unit. The models, with overall width indicated by the first two digits, are the 3601 (36 inch), 2401, and 1601. They differ in stock thickness acceptance and power requirements as well as width. The smallest model is useful with lightweight routers (¾ horsepower minimum), and the others require heavier routers (1½ horsepower minimum). The largest unit will accept stock from ⅝-inch to 1¼-inch thick, while the middle unit takes stock from ⅜-inch thick. The small model is limited to stock ³⁄₁₆-inch to ⅝-inch thick. So probably the middle model would be best for most woodworkers.

The Keller system offers some very good features. Because they are fixed-pin units, they are simple to set up. The use of two templates simplifies setup of each even more, though it does increase cutting time minimally. Pin spacings remain at three inches for the big unit, 1¾ inches on the middle unit, and 1⅛ inches on the small set.

You mount the templates to a backing board of your choice. Mounting holes (already drilled) are slightly oblong, and allow adjustment until a test joint fits perfectly. I suggest using a fir or pine backing board with the two larger units. Hardwood looks good, but because of the size needed, weight gets to be a problem when changing from one template to another.

The workpiece is clamped, upright, in a bench vise: you will need a good, solid bench vise for this work—and a solid bench. I've mounted a Jorgenson ten-inch model to my assembly bench that works beautifully.

Set the tail template on top of the board, and position it to produce tails where you wish them (Illus. 2.67). Clamp the backing board to the workpiece, and rout carefully, moving from left to right (Illus. 2.68). Once the tails are cut, use them to mark the pin board. Set the pin template on the marks (Illus. 2.69). Clamp and rout (Illus. 2.70).

With any soft metal template, it is important to rout carefully. These units should never wear out, unless you strike the template with the router bit, which chews right through the aluminum. Keller supplies carbide-tipped bits which will cut through as though they never even noticed the soft aluminum. In most cases, you can prevent any problems simply making sure that you are engaging the template with the template guide at the start and that the bit is no longer rotating at the end before you lift the router.

Illus. 2.69 Set up to cut pins. (Courtesy of Keller & Co.)

Illus. 2.67 The template mounted and ready for tail cutting. (Courtesy of Keller & Co.)

Illus. 2.68 Cutting tails. (Courtesy of Keller & Co.)

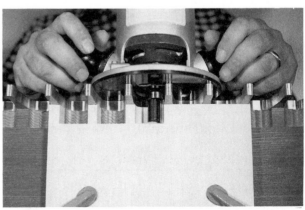

Illus. 2.70 Cutting pins. (Courtesy of Keller & Co.)

Illus. 2.71 This router table offers a unique, adjustable fence, among other features. The mitre gauge groove fits a Delta mitre gauge.

Router Tables. Router tables may be bought (Illus. 2.71) or built (Illus. 2.72). The building is not particularly difficult, as you will note from the plans provided (Illus. 2.73).

Some of the same bits that are useful on a router table may also be used, with great care, freehand, but others are not suitable for freehand use. Freud's box joint bit is a case in point. It requires a powerful router to work well and has a strong tendency to throw the work, or jerk the router around. It is far safer to use the bit only in a router mounted in a table.

Extra-Heavy-Duty Router Table

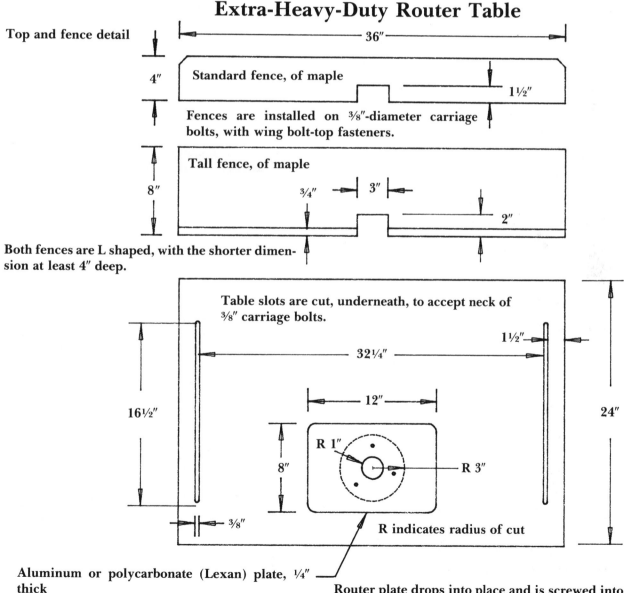

Aluminum or polycarbonate (Lexan) plate, ¼″ thick

Illus. 2.72 Router table top plans.

Router plate drops into place and is screwed into brass screw inserts at each corner, inserts set in 1½″ from each edge, using brass flathead machine screws.

Other router bits may be used freehand, but they do a far smoother job on a router table. **All safety rules, regardless of the bit used, need to be observed.** Larger bits need more care, as do more powerful routers. When using any large bit with a plunge router, check to see that the bit doesn't spread wider than the opening in the metal base of the router. If it has such a spread, do **NOT** use it with that router, as any retraction of the bit will cause it to strike the base of the router.

Dadoes with the Router. Dadoes are quickly and readily cut with routers. There are all sorts of jigs possible for making sure the spacing is proper, but the simplest one is a set of spaced guide bars inside of which the router moves (Illus. 2.74). The space between the guide bars needs to equal the width of your router base. Under the side guide bars are end bars equal to the width of the router base plus the width of the guide bars. Use straight one-by-three or one-by-four stock for all pieces. Make sure the corners are square. Screw and glue the assembly to assure long term use.

Butt the jig on the side of the board to be dadoed. Clamp lightly at the end away from where you'll start cutting. The first cut will produce a dado in the jig's end spacer; mark the middle of that dado. That mark makes alignment for succeeding dadoes easy (Illus. 2.75). Set the depth carefully. Start the router and run it across the piece being cut. The guide bars need to be longer than the stock being cut. Just because you are routing a single 12-inch wide piece,

Extra-Heavy-Duty Router Table

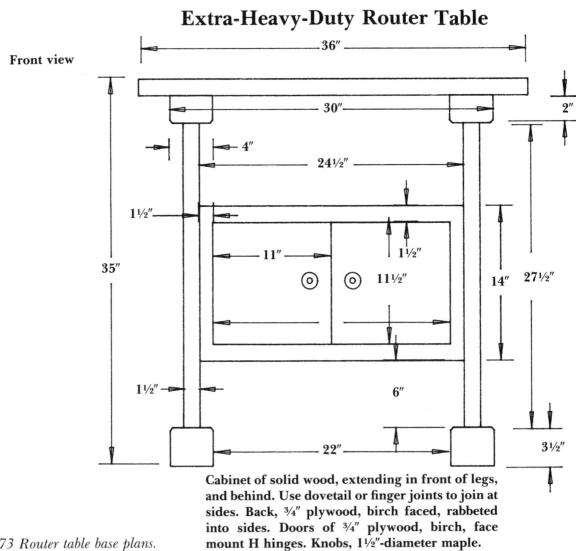

Front view

36″
30″
2″
4″
24½″
1½″
11″
1½″
11½″
35″
14″
27½″
1½″
6″
22″
3½″

Cabinet of solid wood, extending in front of legs, and behind. Use dovetail or finger joints to join at sides. Back, ¾″ plywood, birch faced, rabbeted into sides. Doors of ¾″ plywood, birch, face mount H hinges. Knobs, 1½″-diameter maple.

Illus. 2.73 Router table base plans.

don't count on that being the widest you'll ever cut. It is often easier to match pieces—for bookcase sides and other projects—if all the cuts are made on all the pieces at the same time. Making the guide bars at least three feet long is a good idea.

Using Biscuit Joiners. Biscuit joiners are also known as plate joiners. The "biscuits" or plates are flat and football shaped, 0.148-inch thick regardless of width. The saw-blade tool cuts a kerf that is 0.156-inch thick, a loose fit (Illus. 2.76). The plates absorb water from the glue and rapidly swell to over 0.160 inch.

The biscuit joiner in portable form hasn't been around very long, but it has been around longer in Europe than in North America. The biscuits go back to 1956, when a company named Lamello began making them. Within 13 years, the company was manufacturing a portable groove-milling machine for the biscuits.

Illus. 2.75 Wide dado being cut with multiple passes of the router requires repositioning of the jig for each pass.

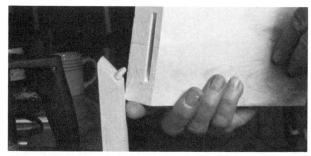

Illus. 2.76 Biscuit being installed in a cut.

Dado Jig For Router

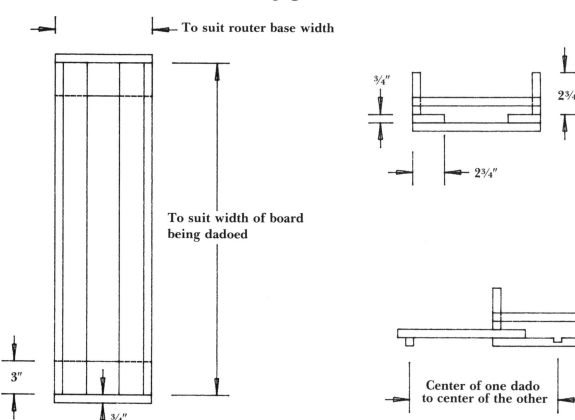

To suit router base width

To suit width of board being dadoed

3"

3/4"

3/4"

2¾"

2¾"

Center of one dado to center of the other

Illus. 2.74 Dado jig plans.

Step guide offers freedom from measurement after first dado is cut.

All of the models from European companies have a number of things in common, including what I consider to be one of the most awkward handle setups found on any tool. Added to this is a propensity for extreme noise—all the machines from Europe *exceed* 100 decibels (A scale), a level that is rough on the hearing.

Porter-Cable came out with a version that solves handling problems and significantly reduces the noise problem. The Porter-Cable 555 model is—by far—the quietest portable unit I've come across on the market, because it is driven by a belt instead of helical gears. The belt drive allows a different shape as well as quieter operation, so that, in general, the Porter-Cable 555 is one of the easiest to handle and one of the more inexpensive.

All of these work with three biscuit sizes, and thus come close to replacing dowels in wood joinery.

Accuracy of jointing is far better with biscuits than it is with dowels. What you are trying to achieve is far easier to attain: the slot cut to accept the biscuit will allow adjustment along the length of the biscuit, while a dowel pegs you to a point and keeps you there. If you've drilled your dowel holes a fraction of an inch off, your project will be a fraction of an inch off without any room for adjustment. With biscuits, you'll never be much more than a small fraction off because of the way the joiners are made. If you are, you can slip things around until the mate is perfect.

The biscuits are of solid beech—stamped to size after being sawn into laths. There seems to be no major difference between the biscuits without brand names, and those with brand names. It makes sense to use the least expensive available when the only other difference is a brand name.

Biscuit Joints. Biscuits are used to join surfaces, substituting for splines or dowels, and usually making for a neater, quicker job. Gluing is simple: glue is best dribbled down along the sides of the slots after a screw-

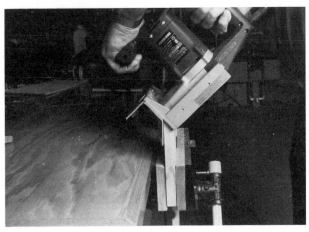

Illus. 2.77 Cutting a biscuit slot in a mitred piece.

driver or knife has been used to remove chips from the slots.

As with any joint preparation, the wood piece must be cut accurately, with ends square—or mitred—as needed for the junction to be made. The better the overall preparation, the better the resulting joint (Illus. 2.77).

Cuts are aligned using marks on the joiner. (My joiner is the Porter-Cable 555, which operates a little differently—especially with mitres—than the others because of its different handle and blade-drive system.)

The joiner has a mark that extends up the front of the faceplate. This indicates the middle point of one's work with the biscuit joiner. Lining this mark up with one board, and then with a second, ensures that those boards will line up easily after the cuts are made.

Edge-to-Edge Joining with Biscuits. Mark where you expect to need the biscuits to add strength to the joint: this will be at eight-inch or wider intervals, for edge-to-edge joining.

Work with two boards at a time, no matter how many you're joining. Mark the boards in two inches from their ends, and about ten inches apart between those marks. Place the cutting guide so that the slot is cut about halfway down the board's thickness. Cut at the marks on both boards. If necessary, clean out the grooves. Insert biscuits and check the joint.

Disassemble the practice setup. Apply the glue, and insert the biscuits for the final assembly. Clamp the boards together, in proper alignment. When the glue has set, repeat the process on the next pair of boards.

Final preparation of the resulting wide board is simply light sanding. This sanding will take less time than for most other edge-to-edge glued joints.

Corner Joining with Biscuits. It is in joining corners that biscuit joinery really excels: the ease, speed, and consistently good results may have you flinging all sorts of dowelling jigs in the trash.

Again, align the pieces, but this time the top piece should have the end of the board facing you, sitting flush on top of the end of, and at right angles to, the bottom board. Make your marks two inches in from the ends, and then at intervals of four to six inches between those.

Cut the slots, starting with the face board. Then go to the end of the other board. You will find yourself cutting into the end piece with little to brace the joiner for most models except the Porter-Cable 555. Line up some bracing material.

Test fit with dry biscuits. Disassemble, add glue, and reassemble with clamps.

T Joints Using Biscuits. Joining internal parts with butt joints is simply done, but requires a few more steps to keep the job manageable. First, when marking to the middle of a ¾-inch board, mark on the ⅜-inch line—always work to the same side of that line. Second, when boards are marked for a particular place, it is a good idea to key mark them so that they return exactly to that place for the practice assembly as well as for the final, glued assembly. If they're not marked, and the piece is at all complex, several pieces will no doubt end up in the wrong places.

Mark and cut the vertical slots first, after which the horizontal slots are cut. Marking distances (thus biscuit insertion distances) are similar to those for corner joints: come

in two inches from each end, and then set other biscuits four to six inches apart.

If you have trouble in getting all the glued parts together in box assemblies within the 10 or 15 minutes of open working time for standard yellow (aliphatic resin) wood glues, do not attempt to just handhold things together until the glue sets. Get a bottle of liquid hide glue, and use its longer open working time to get a proper assembly—and to clamp the assembly square.

Mitre Joints with Biscuits. Mitred joints help some materials to look far better by providing a finished, all-wood corner appearance. By not allowing plies to show (with plywood) or by keeping grain direction and general appearance more similar (for solid woods and pressed boards), the clean, solid appearance is achieved. As a modified butt joint, a mitre joint offers little strength beyond what any butt joint does, so needs some form of support to provide the durability.

Splines, and dowels, have long been popular for this type of support, with splines the easiest to use. An accurately cut mitre joint is then set on a table saw so that the blade rips a ⅛-inch wide kerf the length of the mitre. The corresponding board is treated in the same manner. A spline is then fitted into the groove with glue, and the unit is clamped together. Splined joints offer horizontal mobility during assembly so that accurate fit is simple, *in that plane*. Dowels offer a difficult fit in all planes, especially once the angle changes from a simple 90° to 90° included—that is, 45° plus 45°, 60° plus 30°, etc.

Biscuits offer adjustment along the same plane as do splines, while they also ease accurate slotting so that there is less likelihood of a misfit.

Produce a square mitre in the proper size as required for the job. Bring the two mitred faces together, and mark two inches in from the ends, and after that at four-inch intervals (for very large carcasses, place the marks at six- to eight-inch intervals).

Change the faceplate to the 45° position. Make the cuts for the biscuits. Dry test the assembly (Illus. 2.78). Disassemble, apply glue, and reassemble. If you have trouble clamping such assemblies, I suggest using a band clamp. Check for square as you clamp.

Illus. 2.78 Finished slots with biscuit loosely placed in one. Also check the fit for the complete assembly.

Illus. 2.79 Small lathe with miniature turning chisels from Woodcraft.

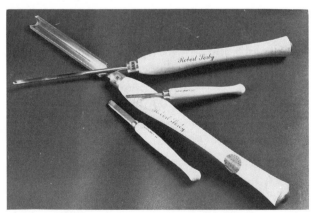

Illus. 2.80 Top-grade, high-speed steel (HSS) lathe chisels greatly ease the work. Woodcraft carries the Robert Sorby brand.

Some Other Useful Tools

A simple lathe can be an extremely handy tool, and, as well, several of the projects call for the ability to turn parts. A small lathe can be used to turn decorative and small parts (Illus. 2.79). Proper sets of lathe chisels can greatly ease the work (Illus. 2.80). A larger, heavy-duty lathe may be required for turning large hardwood legs (Illus. 2.81). A heavy mallet can help in properly setting up the lathe (Illus. 2.82). Choose a good hardwood to practise turning on the lathe setup (Illus. 2.83).

When you encounter a particularly heavy smoothing job, you may find that a power plane is ideally suited to the job's needs (Illus. 2.84). Jointers are also exceptionally handy tools for shaping jobs that require a significant amount of material to be removed (Illus. 2.85).

Illus. 2.81 The heavy-duty AMT lathe, in its initial setup phase. I had to move the entire unit to the left to allow the motor to drop a bit more, increasing tension on the belts.

Illus. 2.82 This weighted rawhide mallet is from Woodcraft.

A set of small tools, such as vise-grips, pliers, wrenches, and a ratchet set, are essential in setting up and maintaining any woodworking shop (Illus. 2.86). Pneumatic ratchets are also very useful around any shop to assemble equipment as well as the projects themselves (Illus. 2.87). I hope these comments on tools will be of value to you as you begin working on the projects that interest you. Keep in mind that many of the projects can be built with hand tools alone. You don't need to run out and buy expensive power tools, if you have some patience and are willing to exert your own energy.

Illus. 2.85 Jointers such as this one can be used to taper a post for the cat bed project. Accessories such as the push block are always necessary to maintain safety with this tool.

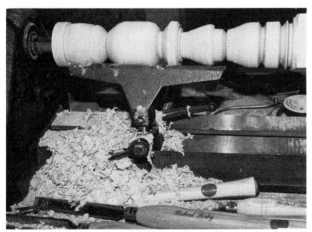

Illus. 2.83 Maple turned cleanly for my first practice cuts.

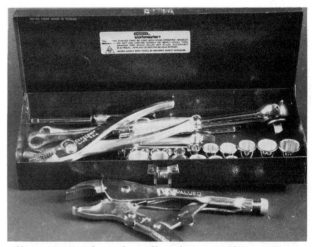

Illus. 2.86 A box of small tools is one thing that you cannot do without in your woodworking shop.

Illus. 2.84 This Skil power plane has a deflectable chip chute so the chips need never be blasted into your face.

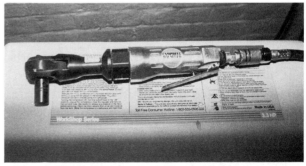

Illus. 2.87 Air ratchets greatly speed any assembly or disassembly job.

3
Gluing and Clamping

For a long period in the history of wood-working, hide glue was the epitome of wood-joining strength (Illus. 3.1). To this day, hide glue is the adhesive of choice for traditionalists for certain jobs. Although there are now many alternatives, hide glue might well serve us all with greater frequency than it does.

Illus. 3.1 Franklin's hide glue. The roller applicator is very handy—available from Woodcraft.

Wood Selection

It's necessary to make sure that the woods you want to glue will successfully mate. Great difference in moisture content from one wood to another will create problems. Similarly, differences in wood structure may also create problems (for instance, teak, with its high silicone and oil contents, does not bond well with other woods—it is even difficult to bond to itself).

The best wide-area glue-ups (especially for sizable laminates, or glued-up flat boards) result when the same species is used. Simply put, all the board is of one kind such as pine—or fir, or oak, or cherry, etc. If part is cherry and part is pine, there will be difficulties, though such difficulties can be reduced by checking the list of gluing properties presented in Appendix C (page 125) to note the expansion and contraction rates of woods.

Plain-sawn boards are best used with plain-sawn boards, and quarter-sawn boards with quarter-sawn. Otherwise, the differences in grain directions will create all sorts of distortion problems over time.

You'll also find it best to allow boards to "temper"—that is, if you are using different kinds of lumber, or the same kinds from different sources, allow all of the lumber to remain at least 24 hours in the environment in which it will be glued.

Selecting a Woodworking Glue

You'll note an array of so-called woodworking glues in many catalogs and ads as well as at dealers. There are not as many true woodworking glues around as one might expect; even fewer are of true interest to the general woodworker. Contact cements, for instance, are of legitimate interest for general woodworking. They can produce a laminate of dissimilar materials. Particular properties of the cement itself allow contact cements to last even when expansion and contraction rates differ markedly.

Woodworking adhesives fall simply into animal (or hide) glues, and synthetics. Animal glues are older, and less used today because the synthetics offer certain properties that they do not. There are as well some properties offered by animal glues that synthetics do not offer, or do not offer as completely.

Hide Glue. The most easily found liquid hide glue today is Franklin's (Illus. 3.1). Drying time is slow, so there's a long window of assembly time for complex projects, allowing adjustments. An added benefit is that the glue is nontoxic.

Hide glues are thicker than most white and yellow glues, resist solvents (other than water) well, and give a pale tan glue line. Hide glues sand well, without gumming. Lack of gumming is important, because adhesives that gum heavily clog and ruin sandpaper quickly.

Synthetic Adhesives. Most adhesives used for woodworking today are synthetics that were formulated specifically for different applications in the woodworking field or drifted over from prior applications in other fields (the epoxies, the cyanoacrylates, the hot melts). Most are types of resin glues that gather strength through chemical reaction or curing. The strength of the cure, as well as the rate, may be increased by increasing the glue line temperature (within certain limits: but, below 120° for all glues).

White glues (polyvinyl acetate resins) are ready to use, and come in squeeze bottles, on up to gallon, and sometimes larger, jugs (Illus. 3.2). Liquid white glues come from many makers. The number of brands is wide, but most are acceptable for general woodworking purposes.

White glues do not offer a chemical reaction cure. As the water in the glue moves into the wood—and into the air—the resin gels. On unstressed joints, you can release clamping pressure in about 45 minutes. Leaving clamping pressure on for several hours is better. Stressed joints must have at least a six-hour set before the clamps are released.

White glues are not always dead white—some are dyed close to yellow to appear more like aliphatic resin (liquid yellow glue). Aliphatic resin glues are more heat and water resistant.

White glues have poor sanding qualities compared to both hide glues and liquid yellow glues. Low heat resistance lets the glue soften, and it gums up the sandpaper, thus creating sanding problems. Low heat resistance also causes a loss of glue line strength at 100° F and above. Water resistance is also low enough so that a high-humidity basement may create separation problems.

The set is fast, limiting assembly time to about 10 minutes—or at most 15 with some versions. Pressure application must be quick, so preassembly of the projects is essential. Fit all the clamps and loosen about a half turn before disassembling. Apply the adhesive, and reassemble quickly with the prepared clamps.

Illus. 3.2 White glue (polyvinyl acetate resin) being applied. Also known simply by the initials PVA.

The glue line is close to transparent once white glue has totally dried. If you have set things up in too cold a shop (below 70° F typically, though I've successfully used this type of glue at 65° F), the squeezed-out glue appears chalky white, and the joint line may be weakened.

Cured white glue tends to give with the day-to-day movement of the wood. This process is known as cold flow and makes this glue undesirable for any highly stressed joint such as structural laminates, where a great deal of bending pressure is applied and released with some frequency. At the same time, the cold flow allows joints to move naturally without creating cracked glue lines or weakening the joint.

Liquid Yellow Glues (Aliphatic Resins). Aliphatic resins were designed as improvements over the polyvinyl acetate resins (the white glues), and do provide enhanced changes in properties (Illus. 3.3).

Heat resistance is a good deal higher, which greatly improves sandability while also improving the strength at 100° F and above. These glues set well at temperatures as much as 110° F, which means that they can be used during some of the hottest summer weather. Raising glue line temperature does increase the set rate though, thus reducing the open window of assembly time.

Yellow glues are less likely to run and drip than the white glues because their basic consistency is heavier. This makes for neater gluing jobs, while greater moisture resistance means that the completed projects may be used in damp areas. Under no circumstances, though, is any yellow glue of exterior quality.

The rate of setting is faster even than for the white glues. This becomes a problem for complex projects—as a general rule, switch to hide glue when project assembly takes more than five minutes. Total cure takes at least 24 hours with the glue line being a translucent pale tan or amber color. Water cleanup—before the yellow glue has set—is possible.

Illus. 3.3 Liquid yellow glue (aliphatic resin) is an excellent general choice for woodworking. It can be conveniently used with an accordion squeeze applicator such as this one from Trend-Lines.

Waterproof Glues

There are a number of waterproof glues now available for use with wood, but the traditional two are plastic (urea) resin and resorcinol resin adhesives.

Resorcinol Resin Adhesives. The resorcinol glues are dark-red liquids (the resins) to which a catalytic powder is added before use (Illus. 3.4). Plastic resin adhesives are highly water resistant, but only the resorcinols are truly waterproof. Where a trade-off is possible, it's more economical to use the plastic resins—resorcinol resin adhesives are about three to four times more costly.

Resorcinols have a fair window of workability, after mixing, ranging anywhere from about 15 to 120 minutes. It is best to go with the longer working life, so check the label. Brush the resorcinol on, or spread it with some sort of spatula (tongue depressors, available at any drugstore, or ice cream sticks from the grocery make great glue spreaders—toothpicks are perfect for small projects). Clamping must be immediate and heavy.

Before starting to bond anything with resorcinol resin adhesive, get everything set up. Make sure that the wood moisture content is below about 12 percent, that joints are tight and fit precisely, and that heavy-duty clamps are ready to go. The clamping pressure needed is high, about 200 pounds per square inch (p.s.i.). One drawback is that the glue line is ugly, a dark red or reddish brown.

Illus. 3.4 Resorcinol glue, in two parts: resin and catalytic powder.

Urea (Plastic) Resin Adhesives. Plastic resin adhesives are dry powders, mixed with water just before use. The resin is urea formaldehyde and produces a highly water resistant adhesive. This adhesive is best used on wood that has a moisture content of no more than 12 percent. The optimum use, and cure, temperature is 70° F.

Plastic resin adhesives are superb for producing joints in projects that have to withstand long-term dampness. Some of these adhesives do well in true exterior applications. They make good general-purpose glues because they work easily in almost every situation, with the exception of high-density woods such as maple and oak. Precise fit of joints is essential, as plastic resin adhesives are not good gap fillers (the best gap filler, other than epoxies, is hide glue).

The rate of setting of the glue is affected by temperature, so complex assembly jobs must be left for times of relatively cooler temperatures. The window of workability ranges from one to five hours. Clamp pressure needs to be in place for at least nine hours. Use moderate pressure. Check that the squeezed-out glue is cured hard before backing off on the clamps. The joint line appearance is good, with a light tan color, and gumming is not a problem since the adhesive resists heat well.

Epoxy Adhesives. Like resorcinols, epoxies are two-part adhesives, but with a liquid hardener rather than a powder added to a liquid resin (Illus. 3.5). Curing is by a chemical reaction, with heat given off as the reaction takes place.

Mix only small quantities at a time when using epoxies (Illus. 3.6). It is easier to work with that way, and waste is costly.

Epoxy doesn't shrink at all as it cures, so it is a good gap filler. Some epoxies are available as putties so that even the largest gap can be filled.

It is not really cost effective to use epoxies for general woodworking jobs such as bonding strips of wood to form a butcher block, or bonding wood for a tabletop.

Another drawback is that epoxies are very toxic, which tends to limit their uses in some shops. Epoxies are messy, but this problem is fairly simply gotten round. Wear thin, stretchy plastic gloves, now available in packs of 100, to avoid the hand mess. Clean up quickly with acetone for any other messiness, keeping the gloves on, and make sure all mixing containers and sticks are disposable.

When your need turns to gap-filling properties for any reason (repair or design), to waterproofing, or to the assembly of outdoor projects, the problems with epoxies are well worth the results.

The required clamping pressure is light; the window of workability is adjustable (depending on the epoxy system) to as much as 90 minutes; gap filling is superb; strength is incredible; and the resulting glue line is either clear or somewhat amber (depending on the brand used).

Illus. 3.5 Slow-setting epoxy, resin and liquid hardener.

Illus. 3.6 Fast-setting epoxy. Mix only small quantities at a time.

Hot-Melt Adhesives. These are quick-setting adhesives that are available to home-shop workers in stick and sheet forms, often with sheet forms supplied as the backing to edging of different kinds. I do enough work with oak plywoods that oak edging in 250-foot rolls, with adhesive already in place, makes sense. This joins easily with an electric flat iron.

The hot-melt glue holds materials for pad cutting, without nail holes. It works well at holding small items in place for routing, too, and is easily peeled off later. Depending on the formulation, hot-melt glues set in a couple of seconds to about 30 seconds. Its best use is for temporary joints because the overall joint strength—regardless of manufacturers' claims—is far lower than that normally required.

A significant drawback is that hot-melt glue is not at all cooperative for sanding. It gums up the paper in a hurry as friction from the sandpaper creates heat. It is easier to slice off any glue residue for cleanup.

Hand pressure is all that is required to get an initial bond, but you'll find things work a lot better if you're in a hot shop, upwards of 85° F. This also warms the wood so that the hot-melt glue doesn't set too rapidly, thus avoiding a poor bond.

Contact Cements. If you've ever built kitchen cabinets, then the odds are that you have worked with contact cement. Contact cement usually doesn't go into the cabinets at all (however, the recent so-called European styles, with laminates over wood substrates, do use contact cement over almost the entire cabinets). More typically the contact cement is used for the countertop where plastic laminates such as Formica are glued to wood substrates.

Ordinary shop-use contact cements come in two basic types. One uses a water solvent, whereas the other uses a nonflammable solvent base such as the solvent 111 trichloroethane (as in Safe Grip from UGL). Some professional types do still use flammable solvents—avoid these completely: they aren't in any way worth the risks involved.

Even for the newer solvents the vapors can be harmful, so make sure you work with proper ventilation. Caution is best exercised with any contact cement, since some water-based solvents can produce fumes that are pretty rough and a few solvents still may not be any too safe around open flame, either: always check.

Contact cement gives a quick bond that allows cleaning up and trimming of the final project right away. Its use is quite simple. Coat both surfaces with the cement, using a brush or a roller. Let the surfaces become dry to the touch. Place the pieces together; for instance, apply the laminate on the substrate. The bond is instant, so proper alignment is critical. Roll or tap over the entire outer surface adjacent to the bond to make sure that the approximately 50 p.s.i. needed for a good bond is achieved.

Since the materials cannot be moved once they are placed together, various methods have come into use to make sure parts are positioned correctly. A slip sheet of Kraft paper or of waxed paper may be used that covers the entire surface about to be bonded. Leave enough paper to grip outside the two pieces being joined; bring the top piece down; align the two pieces; and slowly start slipping the paper out. Once the paper is pulled out about two or three inches, roll or tap over the cleared area to assure a good bond. Pull out the paper the remainder of the way. Roll or tap to assure the complete bond is made.

Choosing Glues

The selection of the appropriate glue for the particular use or project is important, but the proper application of the glue and the clamping of the parts are equally as important. Keep this in mind as you read through the following guidelines for glue selection.

If the assembly is complicated, choose hide glue over any of the synthetics. If moisture is a problem, but only moderately so, go with a urea (plastic) resin glue.

For general uses the liquid yellow glues (aliphatic resins) and the white glues (polyvinyl acetate—PVA—resins) are fine. The white glue is most suitable for longer assembly times (Illus. 3.7), and the yellow glue is typically used for better moisture resistance, better sanding, and better gap filling.

For the best water resistance, select either epoxy or urea (plastic) resin adhesive. Select urea (plastic) resin first, unless the epoxies fill some other need—gap filling, etc. Epoxies are not really cost effective enough to be general-use glues.

For actual waterproofing, use the resorcinol resins. Although these adhesives are relatively expensive, difficult to apply properly (requiring very precise fitting joints), and generally ugly, they are impervious to water.

Most of these adhesives can be applied with either a brush, a stick, or a roller. An all-purpose adhesive is even available as a spray, offering convenience and versatility (Illus. 3.8). Clean off any dust, oil, old glue, loosened or torn up grain, and chips. A test assembly is always a good idea, because once the glue is applied, correcting any mistakes is messy if not impossible. If the glue sets, the mistakes remain.

Applying Pressure With Clamps

Clamping pressure on a glue joint does three jobs. Wood surfaces must be brought into close contact with the glue, while the glue itself is pressed into a smooth, thin, continuous film. The joint must also be held firm once those jobs are carried out.

The clamping pressure required varies with glue type, but it is adjusted according to the glue thickness and wood type. The heavier the glue, the more clamping pressure required; while thin glues need less clamping pressure. Try to achieve a thin, smooth glue line, not a joint that is squeezed dry, which occurs when too much pressure is used.

Illus. 3.7 The boards are ready to assemble, edge to edge into a wide plank, using white glue. Test assemble the pieces first, and make sure the clamps are preset at a point where they can be firmly tightened almost instantly.

Illus. 3.8 Spray adhesive is useful for many things, from tacking plans onto wood to tacking pieces of wood together for pad cutting.

Most woodworking glues used on soft woods will fall in the middle thickness range, requiring clamp pressures of about 100 to 150 p.s.i. Dense hardwoods may require pressures up to 300 p.s.i.

Resorcinol resins require a great deal of pressure, as do urea resins, while epoxy requires little pressure. Avoid excessive pressure in favor of even pressure over an entire assembly. It is better to get even glue squeeze out over the entire unit than to rack the whole thing tight.

Place clamps every eight to ten inches whenever possible. Some lighter types of clamps may need to be spaced closer.

Clamps and Accessory Tools

Woodworking clamps fall into several categories: bar clamps and C clamps (Illus. 3.9); wooden handscrews (Illus. 3.10 and 3.11); and band clamps. Included in these are pipe clamps, picture frames clamps, mitre clamps, and many others. The largest number of variations are found in the bar clamp category.

Illus. 3.9 Bar and C clamps are exceptionally handy, especially inexpensive versions such as these from Stanley.

Illus. 3.10 Handscrews work well on uneven surfaces and at corners.

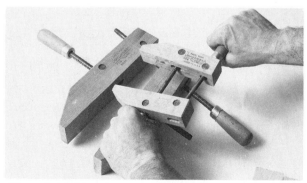

Illus. 3.11 Handscrews adjust quickly if spun hand over hand as shown.

The availability of sizes for bar clamps varies with the weight of the clamp. The heavier the clamp, the longer it can be. Thus normal-weight clamps reach about 48 inches, while light-duty clamps stop at 32 inches.

Band clamps are also available in a variety of units. Stanley Tools' units are about one inch wide and ten feet long, whereas Vermont American's are two inches wide and 14 feet long. Both are excellent tools. Band clamps are for clamping odd shapes, whether octagon frames, chair-leg assemblies, or picture frames.

Short, lightweight bar clamps are a help in some areas that are usually thought of as C clamp territory—gluing up two sheets of plywood, etc. It takes just as many, but there is more depth of throat and somewhat thicker overall clamping possibilities.

Wooden handscrews are great for uneven—as well as even—clamping when marring is not allowed (Illus. 3.10). Handscrews also work especially well to clamp nonparallel surfaces, because they do not creep.

This quick look at clamps misses many types—all handy at one time or another—such as spring clamps (Illus. 3.12) and many of the types of levered hold-down clamps.

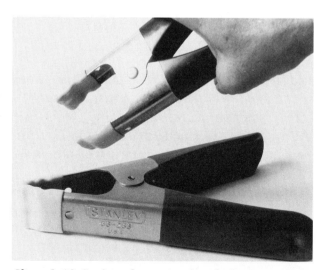

Illus. 3.12 Spring clamps are handy for many light-to-moderate holding jobs—beware that the larger ones for moderate work might even crush light assemblies.

4
Doghouse Plans

Construction may be as simple or as complex as you desire depending on the doghouse you want to build. The doghouse sizes range from those for very small dogs through houses that either will fit, or can be adjusted, to dogs as large as malamutes. You won't find any doghouses with setups for air conditioning, but you will find some that can easily be insulated with insulation board. If you do insulate, be sure to use these newer sheet foam materials and avoid fibreglass insulation. Using the fibreglass kind complicates construction if you want to prevent it from eventually migrating down onto the napping dog).

Some of the doghouses are more easily adjustable to your dog's size than are others. When it's simply a matter of raising a roof or lengthening a wall—as it is for most of these—then the doghouse can be used for any size animal with only a few major dimensions changed. If other more complicated changes would be needed, then try to find another of the plans that will suit your purposes, but with fewer changes.

There are more than a dozen doghouse plans, so one should suit with no or a minimum adjustment. A number of the plans are whimsical. If whimsy doesn't strike your fancy, there are plenty of styles that are more sedate while offering some interesting elements. If what you want is simply a traditional, uncomplicated doghouse, you will find several plans to satisfy your desire.

Changing Materials

Wherever plywood is specified, you can also use the less-expensive oriented strand board (OSB) or waferboard. In fact, when the material will be covered, it is usual to use OSB or waferboard. If either is used as an exterior material, the OSB or waferboard must receive a coat or two of exterior finish of some kind before being allowed any exposure to weather. Even though waterproof glues are used ensuring that the bonding is fine, the wood material itself will change dimensions if it is not protected.

Where two-by-four's are shown in drawings, you may substitute two-by-three's in most situations in which weights are not heavy. Even two-by-two's may be used in some cases.

Changing Sizes

Changing the size of a doghouse is not difficult, fortunately, because the sizes for a given plan may only need few slight variations to suit a particular dog.

Dog House Size Guide

Shoulder Height	6–10″	10–15″	15–20″	20–26″
House part				
Floor	16 × 20″	18 × 26″	24 × 36″	30 × 42″
Side	14″	18–20″	24–28″	32–38″
Door (high × wide)	10 × 6″	16 × 10″	20 × 12″	14 × 24″

The above chart is adapted from a number of similar guides I've noted over the years, but incorporating my own experience in constructing projects for animals.

Remember that everything is adjustable, including this chart: don't take it literally; use it only as a guide for adjustments. Some dogs get fretful in small, tight doghouses, while others love them. Other dogs seem to fret more in larger, over-sized surroundings; so don't neglect accounting for your own dog's behavior.

Some guides work by breed, while others use dog size. I've seen such variations in some breeds that they could almost be taken for an entirely different dog compared to the standard sizes.

Remember that these sizes are suggestions, and are adjustable: heavier, thicker dogs will need more space, while taller, thinner dogs will need, possibly, as much floor space, but less width in doors, etc. Sizes are more or less comfortable minimums.

Doghouse (Stanley Works)

The Stanley Works doghouse is a moderately fancy, medium-sized doghouse that is readily adaptable (Illus. 4.1). You can increase the size if you need extra size—but don't forget to increase the trim lengths as well as the radius of the arc on the door.

The construction of the doghouse begins with putting together the floor, the two side panels, and the two end panels (Illus. 4.2,

4.3, 4.4, and 4.5). The ridge board will go on next (Illus. 4.6). Start by cutting the floor panel to size and nailing it to the two-by-two's that serve as a base. If you haven't bought pressure-treated wood for this use, coat the two-by-two's, at least, with wood preservative to assure durability. There is a ½-inch space between the front edge of the plywood floor panel and the edge of the two-by-two frame. Set the 14-inch strip of quarter-round moulding for the threshold, and then fill the gaps on each side with strips of ½-inch plywood ½″ wide (Illus. 4.7). Cut a 45° bevel along the tops of the side panels, and cut the gable of the end panels at the same angle to patch. For the front and back ends, this 45° angle is most easily laid out with a framing square (the top angle is actually 90° included), but may be done with a combination square or a try square. Use the panel cut first as a pattern for the second one. The rear window is cut with a jigsaw (or bayonet) after corner holes are drilled at the appropriate locations. You can make the cuts with a keyhole saw, if no power tools are available. (Like many of the other projects, this can be built with hand tools alone). The door is also cut with either power or hand tools.

Attach the side and end panels. Nail first to the floor panel, and then to each other.

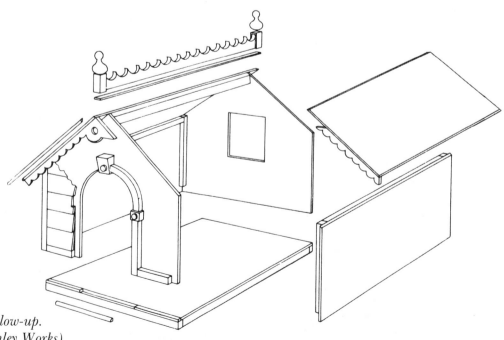

Illus. 4.1 Doghouse blow-up.
(Courtesy of The Stanley Works)

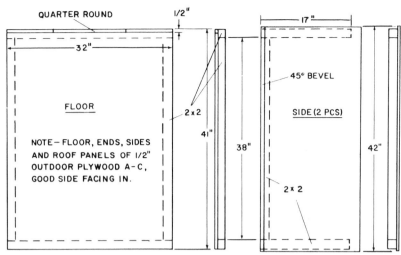

Illus. 4.2 Floor. (Courtesy of The Stanley Works)

Illus. 4.3 Sides. (Courtesy of The Stanley Works)

Materials

Floor, roof, sides: ½″ exterior plywood, A–C
  one floor piece . . . . 32″ × 42″
  two roof pieces . . . . 26¼″ × 48″
  two side pieces . . . . 19″ × 42″
  two end pieces . . . . 32″ × 35″

Framing:
  fir, two-by-two . . . . three 8′ lengths
  fir, two-by-four . . . . one 4′ length

Trim:
  quarter-round moulding . . . . 14″
  pine, 5/4″ × 2″ . . . . 18′
  pine, one-by-one . . . . 4′
  pine, 5/4″ × 6″ . . . . 25″

Siding: 6″ cedar clapboard
  one third of a square . . . . 33⅓ square feet

Ridge and eave trim:
  one-by-four . . . . 45″
  lattice, ⅜″ × 1½″ . . . . 48″
  one-by-six . . . . 16″
  1″ × 1½ . . . . four 24″ lengths
  half-round moulding, ½″ . . . . 17′
  aluminum flashing . . . . 2½″ × 48″
  newel post finials . . . . two, stock

Roof covering: cedar shingles
  one bundle

Base: pressure-treated two-by-two lumber

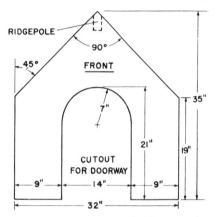

Illus. 4.4 Front. (Courtesy of The Stanley Works)

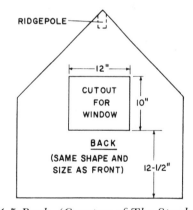

Illus. 4.5 Back. (Courtesy of The Stanley Works)

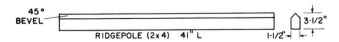

Illus. 4.6 Ridgepole. (Courtesy of The Stanley Works)

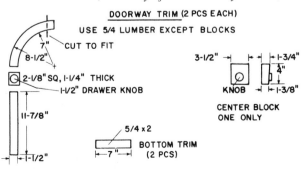

Illus. 4.7 Moulding trim. (Courtesy of The Stanley Works)

Now, shape the ridge board—or ridgepole (Illus. 4.8 and 4.9). It is installed by nailing through the end panels—you might wish to vary this by making the ridgepole about one inch longer, and notching the end panels to fit; then either epoxy it in place, or nail through the sides of the end panels into the ridgepole.

Trim goes on next (Illus. 4.8, 4.9, 4.10, 4.11, and 4.12). Trim must be 5/4-inch material to stand out from the siding properly. A full inch is required: bear in mind that nominal 4/4 (1-inch) stock is actually ¾-inch thick, while nominal 5/4 is only one-inch thick.

Use a compass to lay out the 8½-inch and 7-inch radii on the door trim stock. Use two-inch blocks for trim pieces, planing them down to the proper size. Nail all the trim in place, before you drill pilot holes in the blocks and insert the wooden drawer pulls (newel post finials).

The rear window can be covered with transparent sheet material in cooler climes, or with fibreglass or aluminum screening in warmer areas.

When nailing the corner trim in place, nail the two pieces for each corner together before nailing them to the corner. Cut off the top of each assembly at a 45 ° angle to ensure a snug fit under the eaves. With the corner trim in place, start applying the cedar siding, giving each piece a 4-inch exposure (Illus. 4.13). Once the siding is on—and before the roof panels are added—use end cutting pliers to remove any nails that might have gone through to the inside.

Illus. 4.8 Measuring ridgepole.

Illus. 4.9 Cutting the ridgepole.

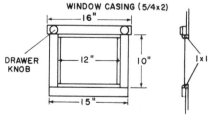

Illus. 4.10 Window casings. (Courtesy of The Stanley Works)

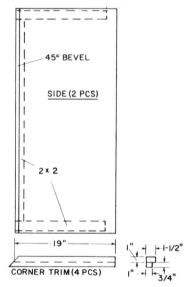

Illus. 4.11 Corner trim. (Courtesy of The Stanley Works)

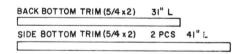

Illus. 4.12 Bottom trim. (Courtesy of The Stanley Works)

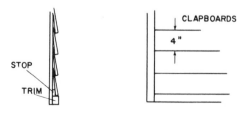

Illus. 4.13 Clapboards. (Courtesy of The Stanley Works)

Bevel the top edge of the roof panels at 45°, and install them (Illus. 4.14). Nail to the side and end panels and to the ridgepole. Cover the meeting joint with the aluminum flashing nailed along the middle and about 2½-inches wide (the edges are left free to bend up over the shingles once they're added).

Next, make the gingerbread (Illus. 4.15). Using hand tools, draw 2¾-inch diameter circles along the edges of the board, making the middle of each about three inches apart. If you prefer using power tools, simply make the marks, and cut the circles with a 2¾-inch hole saw on a fairly powerful drill. The piece is nailed along the middle of the ridge line, with nails driven up through the lattice.

The eave end pieces are cut from a compass-marked board, with circles of 2¾-inch diameter set at a 2⅝-inch spacing. These must be sawed because the design is convex, not concave. Cut four pieces, each about 24 inches rather than the finished 21½-inch length (Illus. 4.16). Hold each piece up against its spot of installation, and then mark it for final cutting. Drive nails down through the edges of the roof panels to secure the trim.

The half-round moulding is tacked around the exposed edges of the roof panels: mitre the joints. Set any visible nails, and fill the holes with wood filler (ZAR). Paint or stain the exterior starting with the clapboards (a clear finish on the cedar clapboards would also do well). The roof covering of shingles can go on after the paint is dry. Start with a double layer, or course, of shingles at the eave. Once the ridge is reached, lift the edges of the aluminum flashing so that the shingles slip under, and the final course's nails are completely covered (Illus. 4.17). If the flashing won't stay down afterwards, coat the tops of the shingles—just under the flashing—with roofing cement, and press down tightly.

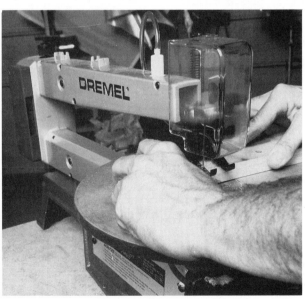

Illus. 4.14 Roof. (Courtesy of The Stanley Works)

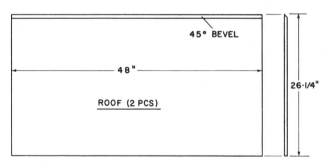

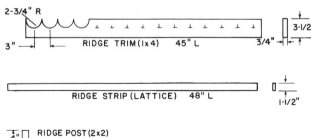

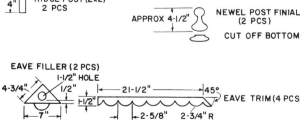

Illus. 4.15 Ridge trim. (Courtesy of The Stanley Works)

Illus. 4.16 Cut the eave trim somewhat long to allow for final adjustment before installation.

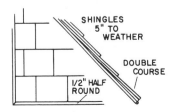

Illus. 4.17 Shingling. (Courtesy of The Stanley Works)

Small Doghouse (American Plywood Association)

If you have smaller dog, you may find that this small doghouse is just right: it is intended for small dogs up to about cocker spaniel size (Illus. 4.18). The construction is somewhat simpler than the previous Stanley Works doghouse, because all of the parts are laid out on, and cut from, a single sheet of four-by-eight-foot APA 303 rough-sawn plywood siding, ⅜-inch thick (Illus. 4.19). If you use thicker panels, then you must adjust the size of the bottom to reflect that thickness.

Draw the pattern on the plywood panel: if you're using a table or band saw, draw the pattern on the face of the plywood. If the saw to be used is a circular saw, or a jigsaw, draw the pattern on the back of the panel (this helps reduce or prevent splintering on the visible side).

Make sure you leave an allowance for kerfs at each cut!

Make the cuts as needed. Start by nailing cleats to the sides, front, and back of the project. Nail the front and back to the sides, and then drop in the bottom of the dog-house, nailing and gluing it to the cleats. Attach the roof pieces, first nailing the lower sections to the front and back. Place

Illus. 4.18 American Plywood Association's (APA's) Small Doghouse.

the top sections so that they overlap the lower section by about one inch, with their tops butting together at the peak. Fit trim around the outside four corners, and nail that in place.

The chimney is optional, and can be ignored if you'd rather leave it out. If you decide to include it, then assemble the chimney by nailing and gluing the four sides to form a box. Nail and glue top trim in place, and position chimney where desired on the roof.

Place the ramp in the doghouse entrance, and nail it to the floor.

Finish the entire project with stain or paint as desired.

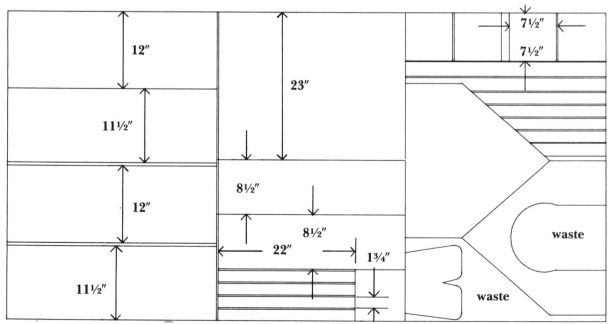

Illus. 4.19 The plan lays out on a single sheet of ⅜-inch APA 303 roughsawn plywood siding.

Doghouse with Interior Baffle

In cooler areas, this shed-style doghouse with interior baffle will provide more protection for your dog against winter winds. By simply adding a rear window that opens and has a shutter, you could also allow a breeze to add more comfort in warmer weather. The door is set to one side, and a wall is placed down the middle of the doghouse, with the middle part of the wall cut away (Illus. 4.20).

Overall, this gives good protection from direct wind, particularly if care is taken in siting the doghouse so that the prevailing winter winds don't blow in the door (a precaution that should be taken in most areas with any doghouse).

A base of pressure-treated two-by-fours laid flat should be constructed under the floor to keep it off the ground. Frame the two-by-fours on a 16″ center (or as close as possible given the dimensions of the floor). Use construction adhesive and galvanized nails to attach the floor. Use the two-by-two lumber for corner posts, with the tops cut about an inch short of the front and back wall heights.

Attach the sides with nails and glue. Apply exterior trim along the base, the corners, and the roofline.

There are two ways to construct the roof. Simply nail on a piece of ½-inch (or ¾-inch,

Materials

Floor, roof, sides, baffle: ½″ exterior plywood or waferboard
one floor piece . . . . 32″ × 36″
one roof piece . . . . 37″ × 41½″
   (Use ¾″ sheet for roof if over 6-foot square)
two side pieces . . . . 32″ × 26″ to 30″
interior baffle . . . . 30½″ × 25¼″ to 29¼″
   (Interior baffle cutout is 20″ × 21″)
one front piece . . . . 30″ × 36″
one back piece . . . . 26″ × 36″

Corner bracing: two-by-two lumber

Trim: one-by-two and one-by-three pieces

Base (not shown): pressure-treated two-by-four lumber

Insulated roof (optional):
waferboard, ¼″ . . . . cut to fit
one-by-three lumber
foam insulation board, ¾″
   (Corrugated aluminum roofing can also be added)

if larger than six foot square) plywood or waferboard. If you want to insulate the roof, cut one piece of ¼-inch waferboard to size, and use one-by-three lumber to frame around the outside edges. Inside that frame, lay ¾-inch thick foam insulation board, gluing the insulation to the waferboard. The waferboard can be nailed to the one-by-three's, or it can be nailed and

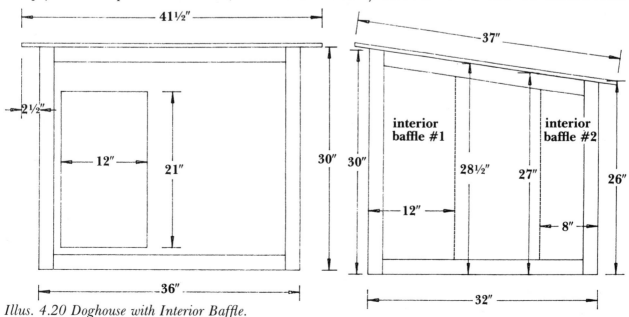

Illus. 4.20 Doghouse with Interior Baffle.

glued. Use corrugated nails to join the frame corners, before you nail the waferboard to the frame. A second piece of waferboard nailed and glued to both the frame and the insulation covers and protects the insulation. The edges of the roof can be covered with one-by-two lumber cut to fit. Mitre the corners of this edging lumber.

Once the structure is assembled, finish the exterior with a stain or paint, to suit, perhaps using a contrasting color on the trim pieces.

The roof can be simply left as plywood or waferboard, as desired, because of the slant. The shed look, though, can be enhanced by fitting corrugated aluminum roofing over the shed roof—don't use corrugated roofing without the wood shed roof since heat loss in winter would be extreme as would the heat gain in summer.

Western False-Front Doghouse

Adding a bit of playfulness to the basic shed-style structure, this doghouse sports a false front reminiscent of the Old West of the U.S. There is plenty of room for you to use your imagination in decorating this doghouse (Illus. 4.21). If having your dog frequent a saloon is not to your liking, then perhaps some other structure common to the towns of the Old West would be better such as the sheriff's office, the newspaper, or the general store (Illus. 4.22).

Start by cutting the front and the two sides (Illus. 4.23). The back fits outside the side walls, as does the front. Cut out both the back piece and the roof. The roof fits over the back and side walls, while it butts up against the front. The top of the back wall should be cut at a 10° angle to allow it to fit properly under the roof. Cut the door and windows (if any) in the front to size, and cut out the top semicircles (Illus. 4.24). In warm areas, you find that actually cutting out the top window will help with ventilation. A good arrangement for this top window is to make it an opening, or partially opening, window with shutters.

Illus. 4.21 Western-style Doghouse front, one idea.

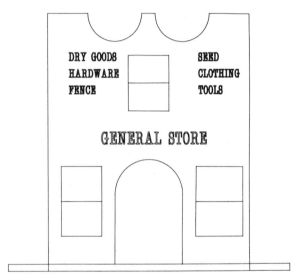

Illus. 4.22 There are any number of possibilities for the false front's design.

Materials

Floor, roof, sides, front, back: ¾" exterior plywood, B–C or better
one floor piece . . . . 38″ × 42″
one roof piece . . . . 30″ × 31⅜″
two side pieces . . . . 30″ × 24″ to 30″
one front piece . . . . 30″ × 36″
one back piece . . . . 24″ × 30″

Butt-joint bracing: one-by-two lumber

Base (not shown): pressure-treated two-by-four lumber

Begin assembling the sides to the front, and then add the back piece. Add a support strip of one-by-two lumber along the front piece as an aid to the butt joint where the

10

roof meets the front piece. Caulk inside and out while assembling (see page 70, Illus. 4.41 and 4.42). Use the 4d finishing nails for assembling the main pieces.

Cut the floor piece, and assemble a frame from pressure-treated two-by-four lumber laid flat with 16-inch centers (or as close as possible) to keep the floor off the ground. Use the corrugated fasteners to hold the pressure-treated frame together until the floor is nailed in place.

Place the assembled structure on the floor piece and position it as desired. Mark the position and transfer the measurements to the underside. Turn the assembly on its roof and set the floor in place, lining up the marks on the underside. Nail the floor in place, also using construction adhesive. Then nail the floor, again using the construction adhesive, to the pressure-treated frame.

Finish the project as desired.

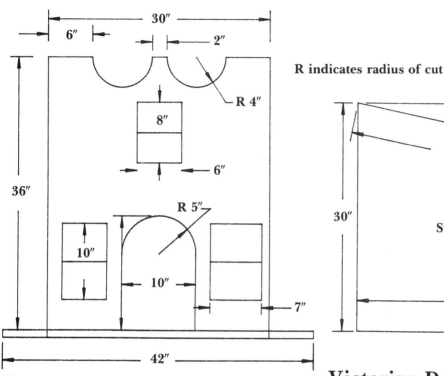

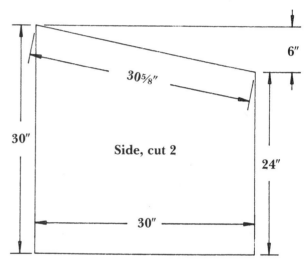

Illus. 4.23 Western False-Front Doghouse plans.

Illus. 4.24 Circular designs are best cut with a jigsaw.

Victorian Doghouse

This small-to-medium-sized doghouse is simple to build and can be either left plain or decorated with gingerbread to give it that period appearance (Illus. 4.25). The windows may be painted or actually cut out, as you wish—a transparent sheet should be added for cold regions, or fibreglass screening for warmer.

Construction is basically plywood, with decorative touches added either by gluing and nailing on gingerbread or by highlighting with paint. Lay out the front and back pieces by drawing a midline 12 inches from each side and using a framing square to get the 90° top angle. You can draw two lines at 45° to the midline, and check the 90° angle with the square. Cut a 16-inch by 8-

R indicates radius of cut

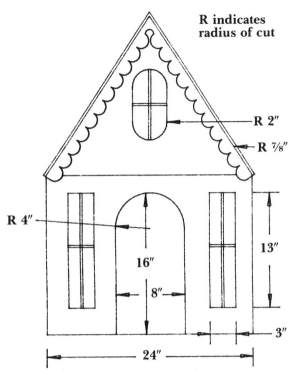

R 2"

R ⅞"

R 4"

16"

8"

13"

8"

3"

24"

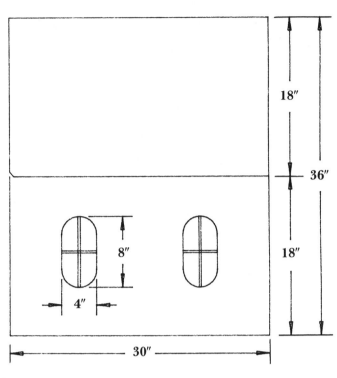

18"

36"

18"

8"

4"

30"

Illus. 4.25 Victorian Doghouse plan.

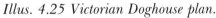

inch arched door in the front as shown in Illus. 4.25. If you like, you can cut a 4-inch by 8-inch window in the back piece.

Cut the two sides, bevelling the top edge of each at an appropriate angle so that they will fit snugly under the roof eaves.

Cut the floor piece, keeping in mind that this piece fits *inside* the front, back and side walls.

The roof pieces are cut to slightly different widths to allow for the overlap as they are butted at the top. Cut each roof piece (Illus. 4.26).

Cut the four 24-inch trim pieces from one-by-three pine stock. The pieces are cut slightly long so that after the gingerbread design is cut, they can be held up to the eaves at the gable ends to mark them for the correct length, allowing for variations in construction. To cut the gingerbread design, mark with a compass ⅞"-diameter holes, starting the first diameter ½ inch from the edge and spacing them ⁷⁄₁₆" apart. Then use a scroll saw, preferably, or a jigsaw to cut out the design. Sand each piece for a better finish (Illus. 4.27).

Begin assembling the pieces by gluing and nailing the sides to the floor. Glue and nail the back to the floor and to the sides.

Materials

Floor, roof, sides, front, back: ¾" exterior plywood
  one floor piece . . . . 22½" × 28½"
  one of two roof pieces . . . . 22¾" × 32"
  second of two roof pieces . . . . 22" × 32"
  two side pieces . . . . 18" × 30"
  one front piece . . . . 24" × 36"
  one back piece . . . . 24" × 36"

Trim:
  pine, one-by-three . . . . four 24" lengths

Base (not shown):   pressure-treated two-by-four lumber

Ridge and roof covering:
  aluminum flashing . . . . 2½" × 30"
  wood shingles (optional) . . . one bundle or less

Illus. 4.26 Setting up for repetitive crosscuts.

Illus. 4.27 Finish sanders such as this give B-face plywood a smooth finish quickly.

Similarly, attach the front, and then lay on the two roof pieces so that they butt at the top, again using construction adhesive and nails to make sure they remain in place.

As with all of the other doghouses, this one needs to be kept off the ground if you want it to last. Assemble a frame of two-by-fours laid flat and joined on a 16-inch center, or as close to that as possible. Attach the structure to the frame as described earlier for previous projects.

The roof can be left as plywood and simply painted slate grey, or you may want to add wood shingles. If so, start with a double course along the bottom, and going up leave a 4-inch exposure for each course. The top should be covered with a ridge cap made from the aluminum flashing and nailed in place over the shingles.

To finish this quaint doghouse, paint the walls and select a complementary color for the trim to enhance the Victorian effect. You can also add some curlicues around the windows and doors. You might wish to cut an arc of trim to go around the door, starting with a 4-inch radius and making the trim about an inch wide.

Log Cabin Doghouse

This small-to-medium-sized doghouse is easily altered to accommodate larger or smaller dogs (Illus. 4.28). The logs in the drawing are out of scale slightly: it only takes five logs to reach the 20-inch height using standard landscaping timbers. For summer comfort, you need to cut ventilation holes in the gable ends. For a comfortable winter doghouse, you can insulate under the roof or over the plywood floor with foam insulation board.

Start by cutting the floor piece from ¾-inch plywood. Make a base support frame from the pressure-treated two-by-four lumber to keep the doghouse off the ground. For this doghouse, turn the two-by-fours on edge and center the frame across the width—that is, at 21 inches. Glue and nail the floor to the base frame.

Cut enough logs from the landscaping timbers, allowing at least a one-inch overhang beyond where the notches are to be cut. Cut notches about ¾-inch deep in both the upper and lower "sides" of the logs—given that most landscape timbers are about three-inches thick by four-inches wide. The very top and bottom courses need notches on only one side. Cut the notches on a band saw, or by hand with a coping saw.

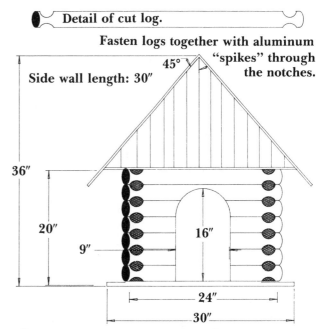

Illus. 4.28 Log Cabin Doghouse plan.

Materials

Floor: ¾″ exterior plywood
    one piece . . . . 30″ × 42″

Roof: ¾, ½″, or ¼″ plywood, OSB, or waferboard
    one of two pieces . . . . 22″ × 30″
    second of two pieces . . . . 22¾″ × 30″

Wall logs: landscaping timbers, 3″ × 4″ × appropriate length

Roof rafters (when ¼″ plywood is used):
    two-by-four lumber . . . . Cut at 45° to fit

Gables: plywood or solid lumber (as desired) to fit

Roof covering (if desired): one of the following
    cedar shingles
    cedar shakes made from cedar shim stock
    cedar clapboard siding (bevelled)

Insulated roof and floor (optional):
    foam insulation board, ¾″

Base (not shown): pressure-treated two-by-four lumber

You may wish to cut the door without the arch. A simple rectangular 9-inch by 16-inch cut would be easier to do, though the arch is easy enough if the logs are already in place, and the construction adhesive between each course had dried. Make the cut using a reciprocating saw, though care is needed to stay on line.

Assemble the logs using aluminum 12d or 16d nails in the notches and construction adhesive (the type meant for decks) along the bottom and top of each log.

Cut the roof pieces making one longer than the other to allow for overlap where they butt at the top. Thinner woods may be used, with proper adjustments for butting. If ¼-inch wood is used, you'll need to frame the roof. In that case, cut two-by-fours at 45° on their top edges to fit. Nail these together, and nail them to the top edges of the walls. You'll need three sets of these roof rafters.

Butt the plywood roof pieces at the top, and nail along the top edge of the walls, or

Illus. 4.29 Boards can be planed down to use for the gables, or plywood may be used.

to the rafters, as needed. Once the roof is in place, you can measure for, cut, and install plywood gables. Or you can use solid wood, if you prefer (Illus. 4.29).

The roof may be shingled or simply painted. Bevelled cedar-clapboard siding makes an excellent roofing material—and adds to the appropriate look of the "cabin."

Let the "logs" weather for at least one season before applying any finish to the landscaping timbers, which are pressure treated.

Platformed A-frame

This house is for small-to-medium-sized dogs, but can readily be altered to serve larger or smaller dogs (Illus. 4.30). To increase the size, for instance, simply lengthen the sides and raise the peak so that the front height and the floor size increase together to maintain the 60° angle of the peak. The platform design is especially suited to hot and/or wet areas.

Begin construction by cutting the four 12-inch long posts from pressure-treated two-by-four stock. Join each pair of these—after the points are cut in the bottom two inches—at the tops with 38-inch base supports. Cut the floor piece, and lay out the front and back triangles starting with the floor's 24-inch width as the base. Measure up from the middle of the base to a point 22½″ up, and lay off a 60° angle. Cut the triangular piece and make a duplicate. Cut a door as shown (Illus. 4.30) 14 inches by 8 inches for the front, leaving the rear wall whole.

Materials

Floor, front, back: ¾″ exterior or pressure-treated plywood
   one floor piece . . . . 24″ × 30″ (or other length)
   front and back triangles . . . . 24″ × 22½″
      (height at peak)

Internal framing (as needed): two-by-four lumber cut to fit with appropriate angles

Roofing materials:
   bevelled cedar siding . . . . 36″ sections
   aluminum flashing . . . . 2½″ width

Platform base: pressure-treated two-by-four lumber
   four posts . . . . 12″ with points
   base supports . . . . 38″ each

Reduced side view: dotted lines are 2 × 4 framing for the A.

If you choose a length over 30″, use internal 2 × 4 framing on 24″ centers.

R indicates radius of cut

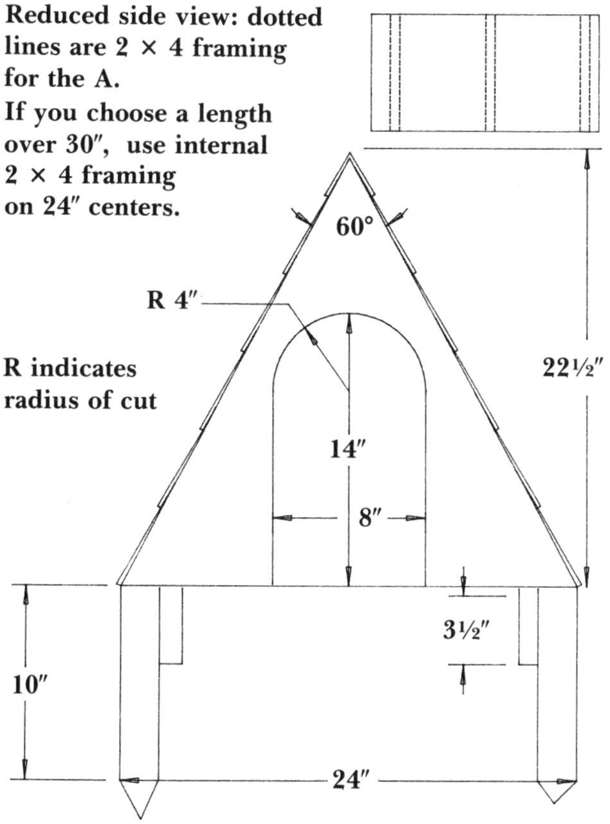

60°

R 4″

22½″

14″

8″

3½″

10″

24″

Illus. 4.30 Platformed A-frame.

Cut at least one set of two-by-fours—depending on the chosen length—to provide a roofing brace. These should meet at 60°, and the bottoms should be cut at 30° to fit properly on the floor. Nail the tops together, and nail the bottoms to the midpoints along the edge of the floor.

Cut 36-inch long sections of bevelled cedar siding for the roof. Run these up each side—leaving 5 inches of exposure on each piece—until they lap at the top, where you should nail on a piece of aluminum flashing bent at the 60° angle.

Drive the base portions of the platform into the ground at the chosen site for the doghouse. Make sure the tops of the sections are level, back to front, and that the sections are level from one to the other. The outside of each staked section should be 24 inches from the outside of the other. Nail through the floor to attach the doghouse to the supports and posts so that it forms its own platform (Illus. 4.31).

Finish the doghouse with opaque exterior stain on the front and back sections.

Illus. 4.31 When nails don't go in correctly, pull with care, using a scrap block under the hammer head. Note the 20-ounce hammer for heavier work.

A-Frame for Larger Dogs

This version of the basic A-frame is kept off the ground by a base frame made of two-by-fours laid flat and held together with corrugated fasteners until the floor is in place. More simply, pressure-treated two-by-fours can be run lengthways and the floor just nailed to those, with no end pieces to close off the floor frame (Illus. 4.32).

Start by cutting the floor piece—it can be longer than 42 inches, but the square area is enough for most dogs. You will want to keep the B side up. Cut the front and back pieces, using the upper angle of 60 ° to set the correct width, even if the width differs from that given here. Cut one piece, either front or back, and use it as a pattern for the other. Cut the door height to at least 20 inches in the front piece, with a width of at least 12 inches.

Cut three sets of rafters from two-by-four framing. Cut the top end of each rafter to a 30 ° angle (this gives an included angle of 60 °). The bottom angle is cut at 30 °, with the opposite slant from the top angle. Allow ⅜″ at the top of each rafter to accommodate the one-by-six ridgepole.

Once all this is assembled on the floor, with the B sides of front and back facing out, you can lay cedar clapboards on the rafters. Nail them in place with shingling

Materials

Floor, front, back: ¾″ exterior plywood, B–C
  one floor piece . . . . 42″ × 42″ (or longer)
  front and back triangles . . . . 40½″ × 42″
  (height at peak)

Roofing materials: one of two options
  internal frame: two-by-four frame with one-by-six ridgepole
    cover frame with cedar clapboards (siding)
  roof base sheet: use ¼″ or ⅜″ waferboard, OSB, or plywood
    cover with standard roofing shingles
    aluminum flashing, for either . . . 6″ width (at least)

Base support: pressure-treated two-by-four lumber cut to fit

nails, and leave a five-inch exposure. When you reach the top, cover the gap with aluminum flashing at least six inches wide, bent to a 60 ° angle.

For a different roof treatment, lay on ¼-inch or ⅜-inch waferboard, OSB, or plywood, and cover that with standard roofing shingles. When shingling, lay the first course of shingles upside down, and come back over those with a course that is set on correctly.

Finish the project with exterior stain on the front and back sections.

Side view

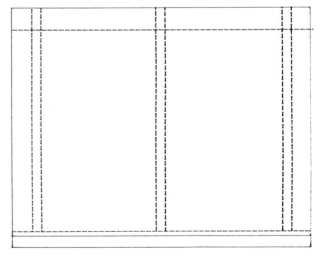

Make sides 4 feet long, leaving two to three inches at each end for overhang.

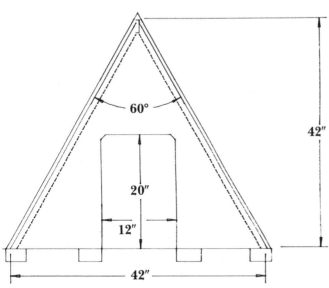

Illus. 4.32 A-frame for Larger Dogs.

Basic, Quick, Plywood Doghouse

They don't come much simpler than this floored plywood doghouse, using only plywood, some exterior corner trip, and some shingles (Illus. 4.33). It is designed for large dogs, but is readily adjusted to fit small- and medium-sized dogs as the construction requires nothing much more than assembling a few plywood pieces with glue and nails.

Start by cutting the floor—the floor may actually be eliminated for smaller sizes—to either inside or outside dimensions. Cut the sides with a 45° bevel on the tops to allow for a smooth meeting with the roof pieces. Cut the front and back pieces with a 90° included angle at the peak—lay out a 45° angle on each side of a midline at 15 inches.

Cut the door in the front piece at least 12 inches wide by 24 inches high.

Cut the roof pieces to allow for the overlap where they butt at the top. Be sure to use ¾-inch plywood: do **NOT** use lighter plywood, OSB, or waferboard on the roof as the span is simply too great for ½ inch or so to hold up.

Start assembly with the floor laid out with the B side up. Position the floor with respect to the front and back walls, and nail those in place, also using construction adhesive. Next, nail one side, and

Materials

Floor, roof, sides: ¾″ exterior plywood, B–C
  one floor piece (optional) . . . . . . 28½″ × 34½″
    (inside), or 30″ × 38″ (outside)
  one roof piece . . . . 32″ × 40″
  second roof piece . . . . 32¾″ × 40″
  two side pieces . . . . . . 36″ × 30″ with 45° bevel
  two end pieces . . . . 30″ × 48″
    (90° included peak)

Corner trim: one-by-two or one-by-three lumber

Roof covering: standard roofing shingles

Ridge cover: one of two options
  standard aluminum ridge cover. . . cut to length
  aluminum flashing . . . . . . 6″ width bent at 90°

then the other in place—with construction adhesive—using the 4d galvanized finishing nails. Set all nails.

Cover all four corners with corner trim using 2d galvanized finishing nails that are then set and puttied over.

Paint or stain the exterior of the doghouse, and then apply standard roofing shingles. Lay the first course upside down, and cover it with a row laid right side up. Continue courses to the top. You may use a short length of standard aluminum ridge cover or a piece of six-inch wide aluminum flashing bent to a 90° angle to cover the gap.

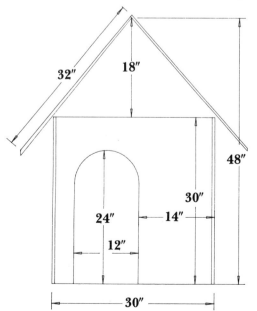

Illus. 4.33 Basic, Quick, Plywood Doghouse.

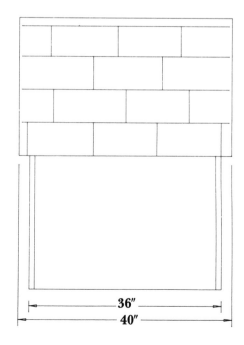

Antebellum Doghouse

The Antebellum Doghouse is one of the semiwhimsical designs (Illus. 4.34). With its chimney and colonnade, it seems as if it might be suitable for certain fancier dogs such as toy and miniature poodles—you may have others come to mind.

Construction is quite straightforward even with the distinctive details. Minor changes will make the doghouse suitable for larger dogs (add about a foot to the sides and increase the door size and you've got it).

Start by cutting the base for the porch and floor. Also make a frame from pressure-treated two-by-fours used flat or on edge to keep the completed doghouse off the ground.

Cut the front and back walls, bevelling their top edges at not quite 45°. Sides are each 41½ inches tall at peak by 24 inches deep. The roofline tapers from 41½ inches at the peak to 33¼ inches at the edges to give you the correct roof angle. Cut the porch roof piece and the two roof pieces—trim to fit later after measuring the assembled base to allow for variations.

Materials

Base, walls: ¾″ exterior plywood
  one base piece (floor and porch) . . . 36″ × 38″
  front and back pieces . . . . 30″ × 33¼″
  two side pieces . . . . 24″ × 41½″ (at peak)

Roof: ½″ plywood
  one porch roof piece . . . . 13⅞″ × 32″
  two main roof pieces . . . . 15″ × 32″
  (trimmed to fit)

Roof covering (optional):
  cedar shingles
  aluminum ridge cap . . . . . 5″ width (bent to fit)
  foam insulation board

Columns: closet pole with larger dowels at base and top
  four main column sections . . . . 24¼″
  overall column height . . . . 28″

Chimney (optional): lighter-weight solid lumber

Base frame: pressure-treated two-by-four lumber

You can paint on the "windows" or use wood strips glued on. Cut the arched door 10 inches wide by 17¼ inches tall. The colonnade that holds up the front edge of the

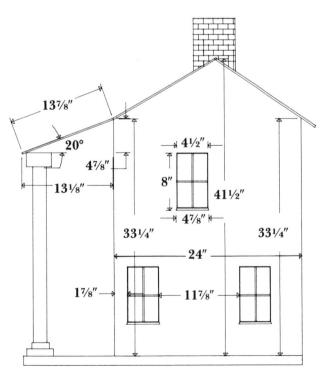

Illus. 4.34 Antebellum Doghouse, as much fun to build as it looks.

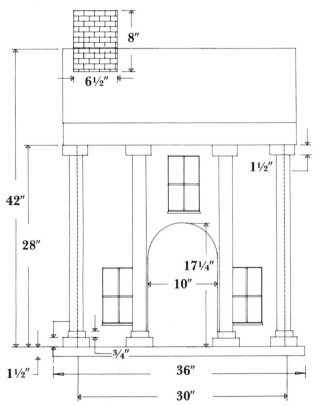

porch roof is made using closet pole for the main column sections with larger dowels at the base and top. The overall column height is 28 inches, with the top slanting up at about 20 ° to meet the porch roof. Cut the largest diameter dowel 1½-inches thick; cut the next largest ¾-inch thick; cut the cap for the columns 1½-inch thick. That leaves 24¼ inches for each of the four main column sections. Shape and sand as desired (Illus. 4.35). Place the two outside columns so that their widest points are just flush with the outside edge of the roof. Position the top inside columns so that their main column sections are about flush with edges of the door opening.

If you decide to include the chimney, use the dimensions on the plan as a guide (Illus. 4.34). You can cut these pieces from lighter-weight solid lumber, and paint and install the chimney assembly as desired.

Start the overall job by cutting all pieces. Then assemble the sides butting inside the front and back. From there, mark the outline of the assembly on the bottom of the base piece, and transfer the measurements to the top. Turn the entire unit over; position the base, and nail and epoxy that into place.

Attach the roof pieces, fitting as you go, with the back edge overlapping the front— but with the back edge still having plenty of overhang. Once the main roof is glued and nailed in place, using 4d nails, install the porch columns. Use a try square to make sure they stay perpendicular.

Illus. 4.35 Belt sanders with a flat top help finish and shape column pieces as you desire.

With all these materials in place, attach the porch roof. If you desire, use cedar shingles to finish the roof, with a 5-inch wide aluminum ridge cap bent to fit.

Paint the completed doghouse as desired. I suggest leaving the shingle roof natural, but painting the roof if it is just the plywood. Do the floor in medium grey, while using a white paint or opaque stain for the house itself.

Colonial Doghouse

This simple, but attractive doghouse, as designed, is for small dogs (Illus. 4.36). For medium-sized dogs, increase the dimensions by half: for large dogs, double all the dimensions.

Begin construction by cutting the two side pieces out first as squares with a starting height and width of 24 inches. Measure 18 inches up the front of each side wall.

Materials

Floor, roof, walls: ¾″ exterior or pressure-treated plywood
one floor piece . . . . 36″ × 36″
one of two roof pieces . . . . 13″ × 33″
second of two roof pieces . . . . 26″ × 33″
one front piece . . . . 30″ × 18″
(30 ° bevel on top)
one back piece . . . . 30″ × 9″
(60 ° bevel on top)
two side pieces . . . . 24″ × 24″
(at peak) to 18″ and 9″

Chimney (optional): plywood or solid lumber, as desired

Roof covering (optional): one of the following
cedar shingles
standard roofing shingles
roll roofing
aluminum flashing (if shingling)

Base frame (not shown): pressure-treated two-by-four lumber

Nails and glue:
4d finishing nails
construction adhesive
slow-setting epoxy (optional)

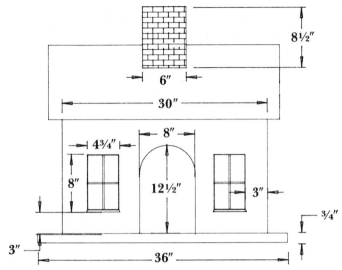

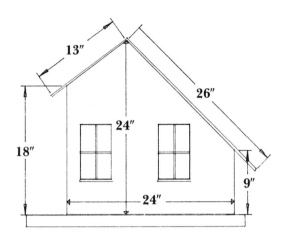

Illus. 4.36 Colonial Doghouse.

Then lay off a 30 ° angle to the 24-inch line. Now, measure 9 inches up from the back edge, and bring a line down from the already set angle to get the pitch of the back roof.

Cut the front wall, and bevel the top at about 30 °, low side facing out. Cut the door 12½ inches by 8 inches wide. Cut the back wall, and bevel the top at about 60 °, low side also facing out.

Cut the two roof pieces. The longer is the back roof. Also cut a floor that is 36 inches square. Make a 36-inch square frame from pressure-treated two-by-fours placed flat side down. Hold the frame together with corrugated fasteners so the floor can be attached.

Assemble the sides to butt inside the front and back walls, using 4d finishing nails and construction adhesive. Square the assembly, turn it over, and mark its position on the base. Transfer the markings to the other side of the base, and position the partially assembled house on the marks. Attach the floor to the base frame, and nail the assembly in place, after applying construction adhesive or slow-setting epoxy.

Place the roof pieces so that the back roof piece butts on top of the front, and nail, again using the 4d finishing nails. The roof can be left uncovered and just painted, or it can be covered with either cedar shingles, standard roofing shingles, or roll roofing. Cedar shingles need two courses at the out-

set, while standard roofing shingles need the first course installed upside down, with the next course laid right-side up directly over those.

Paint on the windows, and paint or stain the house as you desire.

Dog Castle

This doghouse may be just right if you want to add a touch of humor (Illus. 4.37). It particularly suits the whimsical theme—every man's home is his castle; man's best friend's home . . . Construction is fairly easy and fast and painting the masonry look is really quite simple.

Materials

Floor, roof, sides, front, back: ¾″ exterior plywood, B–C
   one floor piece . . . . 30⅝″ × 34⅝″
   one roof piece . . . . 33″ × 36″
   two side pieces . . . . 30⅝″ × 23″ to 20″
   one front piece . . . . 36″ × 24″
      (with extra 7″ tower)
      (See discussion for variations to front design)
   one back piece (not shown) . . . . 36″ × 20″
      (10 ° bevel on top)

Roof butt-joint support: 1½″-wide plywood strip

Base frame (not shown):   pressure-treated two-by-four lumber

Begin construction by cutting the back (not shown in Illus. 4.37). Cut the floor piece keeping in mind that it fits inside the four walls. Cut the roof piece, and cut the sides (as shown) 30⅝ inches deep, with the front 23 inches high and the back 20 inches high (Illus. 4.38).

The front is essentially 24 inches tall and 36 inches wide, but the "tower" sticks up a further 7 inches (Illus. 4.39). The crenellations are ½-inch deep by one inch wide (no more). If they're any higher, the roof will stick up over the edges, not fitting inside properly. To fix this problem for deeper crenellations, make the basic front wall height 26 inches, with the tower still 7 inches high. Then you will have room for the 1½-inch by 1½-inch crenellations I used (Illus. 4.40).

Illus. 4.38 Cutting the castle sides is made easier with a circular saw, because of the angle needed.

Illus. 4.39 Front of castle with door and tower.

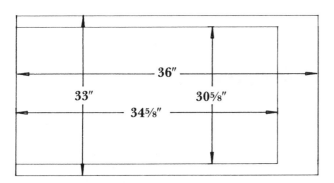

The larger of the two pieces is the roof; the smaller is the floor.

36"
33"   30⅝"
34⅝"

Drawings not to scale.

Back 36″ wide × 20″ high (not shown).

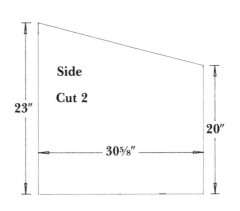

7"
3"
10"
15"
24"
36"

Side
Cut 2
23"
20"
30⅝"

Illus. 4.37 Dog Castle plans.

Make the door cutout 10 inches by 15 inches, or larger. The floor space in this version, along with the height, limits its use to medium-sized dogs, or smaller. Increase the side depth by 12 inches and the height by about 6 inches to use for large dogs.

Assemble the floor inside the walls and attach the front and the back (Illus. 4.41). Place a plywood strip just below the crenellations, plus ¾ inches to allow for the roof thickness. The strip supports the front of the roof. Caulk along this strip and also along the butt joint when the roof is installed (Illus. 4.42).

Stain a Cap Cod grey overall (Illus. 4.43). Use a slender brush to highlight the windows, and to draw an outline in black around the door. The painting for the masonry look is simple. Use the flat grey, opaque latex stain as the background. Draw black lines with the thin brush or a wide, waterproof soft-tipped pen.

As is always the case, place the unit on a base of pressure-treated two-by-fours laid flat. Hold the frame together at first with corrugated fasteners. The frame will help keep the inside of the house from getting too damp in wet weather.

Illus. 4.40 Cutting crenellations.

Illus. 4.42 Caulking along the inside of the front roof support strip. Also caulk along the outside once the roof is installed.

Illus. 4.41 Before roof is added. Note the slight bevel (10°) on top of back wall. This lets the roof sit flat.

Illus. 4.43 Ready to finish.

Gambrel Roofed Doghouse

This design, as shown, is for a very small dog, but it is easily adjusted to larger dogs simply by lengthening various framing members (Illus. 4.44). The original I built wound up being placed on a deck for the use of a family of cats, instead of the small dog it was intended for.

Materials

Floor: ¾″ exterior plywood, B–C
one floor piece . . . . 24″ × 18″

Sides: options, applied to house frame
½″ or ¾″ plywood . . . . cut to size
cedar siding . . . . board-and-batten style

Roofing: applied to roof framing
⅜″ waferboard underlayment
cedar shingles or cedar siding (bevelled)
aluminum flashing . . . . 4″–5″ wide

Framing:
one-by-four stock (mock-up material for size adjustments)
two-by-four stock (vertical frame, rafters and top plates, angled roof supports)
one-and-a-half-by-two stock (bottom framing—sill)

Gussets:
⅜″ waferboard pieces

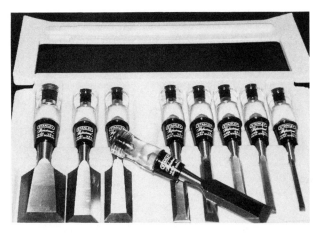

Illus. 4.45 A good set of chisels is helpful in notching cleanly.

Start by cutting the floor piece. Cut the two-by-four corner posts and the one-and-a-half-by-two bottom-framing (sill) pieces. Cut the top plates and rafters from two-by-fours with lap joints cut in each end. Cut the inner wall frame from two-by-fours notched to fit over the sill boards (Illus. 4.45). Frame the door as needed for size.

You can see the ease of fitting this design to different sizes of dogs. Simply increase the length of the framing members and the size of the floor, and go ahead. Some adjustments will be needed in the gambrel roof framing, but those are easily made as long as the angles are maintained (Illus. 4.46). In fact, just determine the width needed, then build a mock-up roof rafter set using one-by-four material cut to fit.

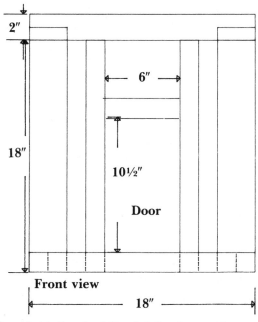

Front view

Illus. 4.44 Gambrel Roofed Doghouse plan.

Note lapped joints

Peak angles, each 60°

Side butt joint has 30° cut for top piece, 60° cut for bottom piece.

120° included

19½″

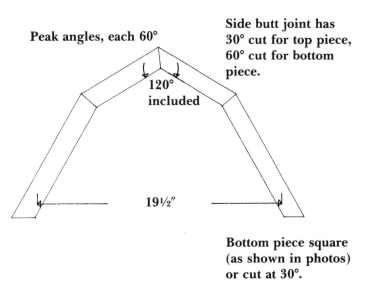

Bottom piece square (as shown in photos) or cut at 30°.

Illus. 4.46 Roof framing and gusset.

The one-by-four material is convenient—and less costly—if you need to make adjustments to get the right combination of angles and lengths. Once you have the proper width to allow the roof to overlap down over the frame, produce the house frame to width and length, as desired. Adjust for length by simply increasing the number of roof framing member sets to suit—making sure the framing is no more than 24 inches on center.

In preparing the roof frame mock-up, cut angles in the one-by-four stock to check the fit: the top of the gambrel roof forms a 120 ° included angle, or 60 ° on each side of the peak. At the side roof butt joint, the top board is cut at 30 °, mated to a board cut at 60 °. The bottom of the lower board is cut at 30 ° if you wish it to be parallel with the ground, or it can be left square. Check each piece for length, and once the lengths are correct, use the one-by-fours as patterns to cut the appropriate number of pieces from the two-by-four stock. Assemble with waferboard gussets, and then nail in place on the frame assembly (Illus. 4.47). Note that this roof pattern comes down over the framing an inch or two, and that you nail through the rafters into the top plates (Illus. 4.48).

Next, install siding. Plywood may be cut to size and installed, or you might do as I did and create a board-and-batten style in cedar. If you decide on the cedar, make sure to get inside and snip off, using end cutters, the ends of all the nails that poke through.

Roofing can be any of a number of items, starting with ⅜-inch waferboard. You can cover the waferboard underlayment with cedar shingles. Instead, you might prefer to use bevelled cedar siding. In either case, leave plenty of overhang at each side junction, and cover the top with a four-to-five-inch wide piece of aluminum flashing bent to a 120 ° angle.

Illus. 4.47 Framing partly assembled.

Illus. 4.48 Frame completely assembled. Note how rafters fit down on the top plates, top plate is lapped at corners, and studs are notched to fit over the sill.

Decks and Doghouses

Rather than presenting a particular plan, here I pass on the useful concept of deck-style doghouse pens that you can apply to any number of dog-housing needs (Illus. 4.49). This was provided by the retired NFL quarterback, Bert Jones, and his brother, who own a wood-preserving business in Louisiana. The deck-style doghouse platforms were designed and built to keep things simple.

Constructed much like any deck, these dog pens and houses give impressive results: in their wet, hot environment, the Jones brothers have healthier dogs, less mess, and a generally happier setup. Possibly the best part is the elimination of odor problems.

Illus. 4.50 The small pen. (Photo by Bert Jones/ Wolmanized Wood)

Construction is simple. Lay out and build following the requirements of a deck, including placing posts in dug postholes and making sure there is allowance between boards for water run off, just as there is with any deck. Construct doghouse(s) on top of the decking. The Joneses built several versions, large and small (Illus. 4.50 and 4.51).

Illus. 4.49 One of the Jones' elevated, deck-style dog pens. (Photo by Bert Jones/Wolmanized Wood)

Illus. 4.51 The large pen handles a good number of dogs. The roof, of corrugated metal, leaves plenty of area to allow a breeze. (Photo by Bert Jones/ Wolmanized Wood)

APA Gambrel Roofed Doghouse, with False Skylights

This house offers good height, and some unique features to house your dog in comfort (Illus. 4.52). Assembly is straightforward, and you have the choice of cutting all the parts at once, or cutting as you go along to allow for possible variation.

Illus. 4.52 APA Gambrel Roofed Doghouse, with false skylights.

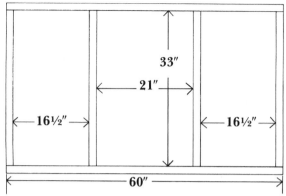

**Cut floor piece
from ½″ exterior plywood, 36″ × 60″**

Illus. 4.53 APA Gambrel Roofed Doghouse, with false skylights: floor frame layout (Courtesy of Marvin Becker).

Start with the floor assembly (Illus. 4.53), and go on to the frame construction (Illus. 4.54), after which the frame is covered (Illus. 4.55). It is a good idea with this house (as well as any of the other doghouses with floors) to create a vapor barrier by stapling a sheet of plastic to the floor frame before the floor piece is attached. Carefully cut the frame and rafter pieces as required. Lay out and cut the rafter angles carefully, and add gussets (metal KantSag S202, recom-

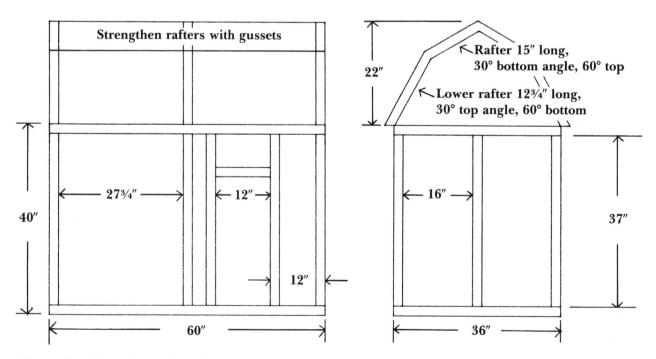

Illus. 4.54 APA Gambrel Roofed Doghouse, with false skylights: house and roof frame layout (Courtesy of Marvin Becker).

mended) before installing the rafters on the house.

Use 4d galvanized finishing nails for the floor assembly. General framing is done with 10d and 12d nails, whereas you can use 4d or 6d finishing nails to add the roof sheathing or siding, if desired. The gussets can be attached with 8d box nails. Use standard one-inch aluminum or galvanized roofing nails to place the roofing felt, and cover each exposed nail with a dab of roofing cement.

Assembly of ¾-inch wood pieces, such as for the skylights, is done with 6d finishing nails. The skylights are for decoration only. If the skylights were real, they'd present a number of framing and possible leakage problems. The inside of the house would also heat up faster, and, of course, allow light in—if your dog wants a nap, a darker, cooler environment may provide better, more comfortable sleeping.

When you are ready to finish the doghouse, the APA's original colors seem a good choice. Barn red was used for the main parts, with the trim simply done in white.

Materials

Floor:
    floor frame assembly . . . . . two-by-four lumber
    floor piece, ½" exterior plywood . . . 36" × 60"
    vapor barrier . . . . . plastic sheet (between floor frame and floor piece, stapled)

House frame: two-by-four lumber, cut to fit

Roof frame:
    rafters . . . . two-by-two lumber
    ridgepole . . . two-by-four, 60" with bevelled top

Frame covering: ½" exterior plywood
    one back piece . . . . 40" × 60"
    two end pieces . . . . 40" × 36"
    one front piece . . . . 40" × 60"
    two gable ends . . . . 40" × 22" (at peak)
    two upper roof pieces . . . . 70" × 14⅜"
    two lower roof pieces . . . . 70" × 19½"

Skylights: make three, ¾" thick wood stock
    two base pieces each . . . . 10" × 5¾"
    four end pieces each . . . . 10" × 2"
    two side pieces each . . . . . 2" width at each end, cut to fit gambrel roof angle

Trim pieces: one-by-three, cut to fit

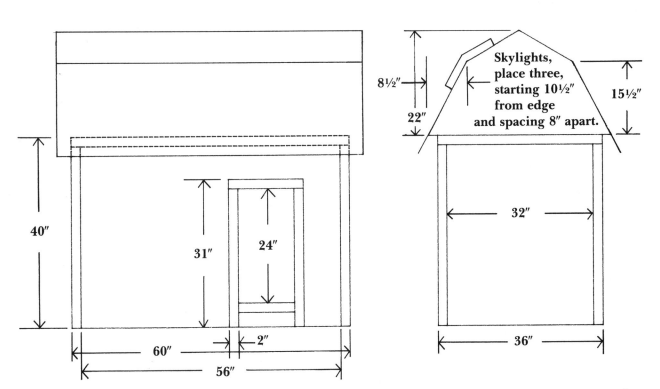

Illus. 4.55 APA Gambrel Roofed Doghouse, with false skylights: frame and roof covering (Courtesy of Marvin Becker).

5
Dog Sleeping Boxes and Carriers

In addition to providing a sheltered house for their dog outdoors, many dog owners find that their biggest needs are providing a comfortable sleeping place indoors and finding some way to get their dog from here to there without having to worry about what's going to happen to vehicle seat upholstery or related items. In this chapter I offer some projects to address these concerns for indoor sleeping boxes and transport.

Carrying cases of steel wire, or molded plastic and wire, are readily available at almost reasonable costs, but the larger your dog, the more expensive these cases become, and the less likely it is that you will have such an item on hand. At the same time, many people simply carry dogs in the backs of pickup trucks, a means of transport that works well for one dog, much of the time. For more than one dog, or for longer trips—or for an excitable dog—some other solution becomes essential: short of converting a pickup truck into a "dog camper," there are often not many options.

Dog Carrier for Pickup Trucks

It's easier to add a removable transport cage to the back of a pickup than to any other vehicle (Illus. 5.1); the range of vehicle sizes increases the range of possible cage sizes as well as the number of dogs that can be carried. Such carriers can be made to hold one dog, or a number of dogs, and may have partitions, or, for dogs used to being together, can be built without partitions.

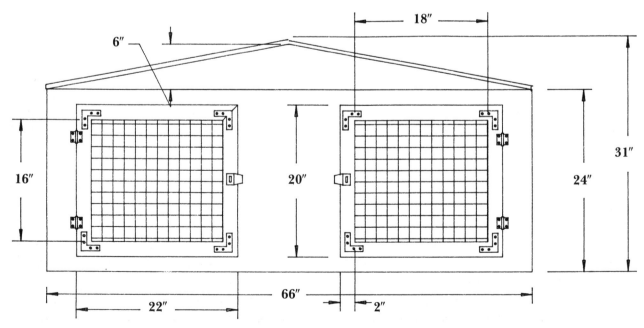

Illus. 5.1 Dog carrier.

Materials

Floor, sides, back, front (partial): ¾″ exterior plywood, B-C
  one floor piece . . . . 66″ × 24″ (as desired)
  two side pieces . . . . 24″ × 24″ (as desired)
  one back piece . . . . . 66″ × 24″ (6″ rise at peak)
  one front piece . . . . . 66″ × 24″ (6″ rise at peak)

Roof: ½″ exterior plywood, B-C
  two overlapping pieces . . . . cut to fit

Divider (if desired): ½″ plywood, cut to fit

Doors:
  one-by-three or one-by-four yellow pine wire mesh, 2″ × 2″
  corner braces, eight, ¾″ × 3″
  hinges, four, 2″
  padlocks and hasps or large hooks and eyes

Fasteners and Glue:
  1½″ drive screws
  1¼″ drive screws
  staples
  construction adhesive

With some size adjustments, similar carriers can be placed in the rear sections of suburbans, station wagons, and vans. However, it's often simpler to construct a barrier between driver and animals than it is to install and remove a cage that can be quite heavy.

This dog carrier can be made to fit nearly the full depth of the pickup truck bed, as required, if the carrier is a single compartment. The two-compartment version with the divider seldom needs to be more than two feet deep, unless the dogs involved are particularly huge—this is for transport, not to live in. If trips are likely to be exceptionally long, then add depth to the carrier.

Cut the floor, sides, back and front from the ¾-inch plywood. The width shown (Illus. 5.1) is 66 inches, which will fit inside the bed of most full-size pickups, but always measure your truck—especially if it is a downsized model. Determine the widths for the ½-inch plywood roof pieces so that they will overlap slightly, and cut both pieces.

Cut the openings for the doors in the front piece. Use one-by-three or one-by-four yellow pine—it is stronger than white pine—for the framing of the doors. Adjust the lengths of the door pieces to allow the original stock width to be used—at least two inches for the one-by-three or 3½ inches for the one-by-four. Strengthen the door frames by using ¾-inch by 3-inch corner braces. Use at least two 2-inch hinges for each door. Secure the door closure with either padlocks and hasps or large hooks and eyes, as desired. Finish the door assembly by stapling two-inch square wire mesh to the backside of each door frame.

If a divider is desired, lay in two ¾-inch square (nominal one-by-one) cleats down the middle of the floor, spaced one-half inch apart to allow for a ½-inch plywood divider. Continue the cleats up the back and front walls. Attach the cleats with construction adhesive and 1¼-inch drive screws. Install the divider by applying construction adhesive and fastening with 1½-inch drive screws.

To help with putting your dog carrier in the pickup bed, and with removing it afterwards, attach rope or steel pulls at the middle of the top front and at the edges

All Doghouse Platform

When a friend not long ago requested a doghouse that was up off the ground to keep the dogs out of our red mud during a particularly wet period—a relief following a too-long drought—I decided that rather than design a doghouse to be set on posts, as was done for the Platformed A-frame (Illus. 4.30, page 63) and the elevated, deck-style dog pens (Illus. 4.49 to 4.51, page 73), I would simply construct a platform on which to rest the doghouse (Illus. 5.2). This design is relatively small but can be easily made wider and to any depth provided the bracing is kept to about 30 inches on center. This simple platform allows you to use any doghouse design even in the warmest and wettest regions.

Cut the top piece from the plywood or, if you prefer, you can construct a platform top using pressure-treated two-by-four or

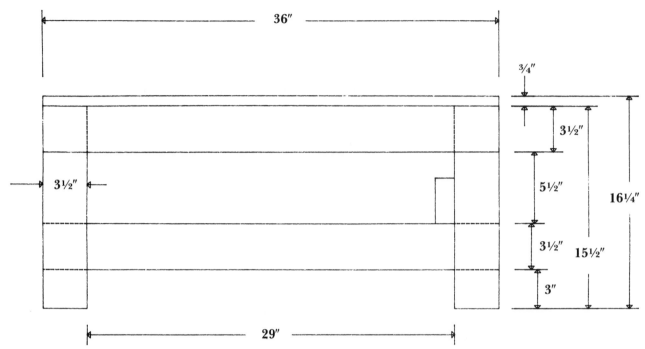

Illus. 5.2 All Doghouse Platform.

Materials

Top: ¾″ exterior plywood, 36″ × depth as desired

Bracing: two-by-four lumber
two upper braces . . . . 36″ length
two upper braces . . . . 33″ length
   (adjust for depth)
three lower braces . . . . 36″ length

Legs: pressure-treated lumber (retention rate of
0.60 lb/ft³)
four pieces . . . . 15½″ length

two-by-six lumber, leaving about ⅛-inch gaps between the boards. Eventually the doghouse will be bolted or nailed to the platform top.

Cut the braces from the two-by-four lumber. Notice that only three braces are required for the lower set. This open side will allow your dog to use the platform as a cool "outdoor" spot to crawl under when the weather is hot.

Cut the legs from pressure-treated lumber and begin assembly. Note also that the legs *must* be from pressure-treated wood that has a retention rate of 0.60 pounds per cubic foot to be suitable for either ground contact or in-ground use.

When your platform is ready, you then have the freedom to provide any design of shelter for your dog without being restricted by the local weather conditions.

Dog Transport Box

This box is designed to be disassembled and stored when not in use (Illus. 5.3 and 5.4). The pieces are attached with machine screws and T nuts so that the pieces come apart separately and can be easily stacked. The top remains attached to the back but conveniently folds down onto the back once the back is removed.

The box shown (Illus. 5.3 and 5.4) is for large dogs, with an overall width of 42 inches, depth of 33½ inches, and height of 29 inches. If the box is to be used as a shipping crate for large dogs, instead of just for short-term transport, increase each dimension by a foot.

While this box is designed to be made with machine screws and T nuts, smaller ones may be made with brass screw inserts and machine screws. The sides are framed in crate style, with a center brace, using the one-by-four yellow pine and quarter-inch OSB, waferboard, or exterior plywood. The floor is framed as well, but is made of

½-inch plywood. The back is framed, and ⅜-inch plywood is used to fill it out. Cut rabbets the proper depth and width for the pieces of plywood to fit in the frame boards: ⅜ inch × ¼ inch for the sides and ⁹⁄₁₆ inch × ⅜ inch in the back. Cut the same size rabbet in the front frame as in the back, but use ¼-inch or larger hardware mesh to cover the frame, and lay in ¼-inch thick × ⅜-inch wide strips to cover the jagged mesh ends.

The frames may be made using mending plates and five-inch corner braces, or you may use half-lap joints.

The top is simply unframed ¾-inch plywood.

Once all the parts are framed, drill a series of holes to fit the machine screws, as shown in the side view (Illus. 5.4). Mark the holes on the sides of the front, bottom, and back. Drill and insert the T nuts.

Assemble the pieces with the machine screws, except for the top. Once everything is drawn up tight, the hinges for the top are installed. The latch goes on last. When disassembling, the top folds down onto the back after the back is removed. The other pieces all come off separately and may be stacked on the back/top assembly.

Rope handles are inserted through holes in the center brace on each side: use ½-inch to ¾-inch rope, and knot the inside ends carefully.

Materials

Framing: yellow pine, one-by-four lumber

Floor: framing with ½″ plywood

Top: unframed, ¾″ pressure-treated plywood

Sides: framed with center brace and ¼″ OSB, waferboard or plywood

Back: framed with ⅜″ plywood

Front screen: ¼″ or larger hardware mesh ¼″ × ⅜″ wood strips to cover mesh border

Fasteners and other materials:
machine screws and T nuts or brass screw inserts
5″ corner braces (as required)
mending plates (as required)
½″ or ¾″ rope for handles

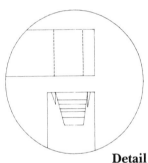

Detail of T nut for sides to bottom, bottom to back, sides to back.

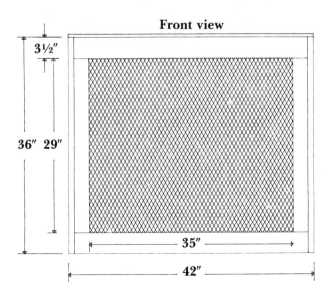

Illus. 5.3 Dog Transport box, front view.

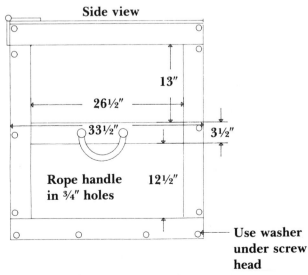

Illus. 5.4 Dog Transport box, side view.

Dog Sleeping Box

Sleeping boxes are easy to construct and help keep your dog's sleeping area clean and orderly, keeping any padding in one place (Illus. 5.5). Also, sleeping boxes can conveniently be filled partially with cedar shavings, which help keep down flea infestations.

This box is made of ¾-inch oak, actually one-by-eight in nominal size, with finger-jointed ends (Illus. 5.6). It is 32 inches square, close to the maximum that can be easily handled on a table saw to cut finger joints.

Make the finger joints after cutting the wood to length, but before cutting the wide notch in the front piece. Dado the bottom edges up to ⅜ inch, making the dado ⅜ inch deep by ¾ inch wide to accept the square bottom piece. Cut the bottom from B-C exterior plywood, and use with the B side up.

Once all of the finger-joint cuts and dadoes are made, cut the wide notch in the front, starting 3½ inches in from each end, radiusing the corners of the cut down to a depth of 1½ inches (make the cuts on an angle as shown in Illus. 5.5, about two inches wide over the 1½-inch drop).

Assemble the two sides, with glue on the finger joints, to the front. Square the corners. Slip the bottom into place—without any glue—and add the final side. **MAKE SURE YOU DO NOT GLUE THE BOTTOM IN PLACE.** The bottom piece is quite

Materials

Bottom: ⅜″ exterior plywood, B-C
large dog . . . . 31¼″ square
medium-sized dog . . . . . 23¼″ square (plywood can be ½″)
small dog . . . . 15¼″ square

Sides: one-by-eight oak boards (¾″ actual thickness)
four finger-jointed pieces . . . . 7½″ × 32″ (or 24″, or 16″)

Illus. 5.6 Finger joints cut in oak for the sleeping box.

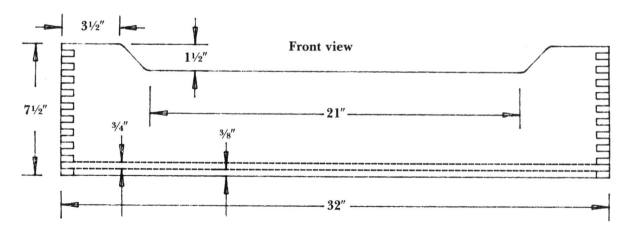

Illus. 5.5 Dog Sleeping Box using finger joints with dado.

secure in the dadoes as long as the finger joints are glued fast, but wood movement will split the joint if the bottom itself is glued in place. If you feel insecure with the piece unfastened, pin it from the bottom using one-inch brads and a nail spinner or pilot holes, with one brad at the middle point of the two opposite sides only. You may also use small screws for the same purpose—a ¾-inch no. 4 is preferable, or perhaps a no. 6.

Sand the assembled finger joints down level and finish with polyurethane. Add cedar shavings, loose or in a sack (in a sack stays neater).

The size is very easy to change on this plan. Simply cut the sides longer, or shorter, as desired. If the sides get down to 24 inches, you can also reduce the bottom thickness—and thus, the dado width—to ½ inch. You'll find that 40 inches is about as far up in size as you can accurately cut finger joints on the table saw. As you increase the size, you may want to nail or glue on a floating brace—one inch wide by ⅜ of an inch deep—across the middle. This is glued and nailed to the bottom piece, but only nailed—not glued—to the box sides.

Simple Sleeping Box

This sleeping box can serve as well as the finger-jointed one, but is somewhat simpler to construct (Illus. 5.7). Rather than the finger joints, it uses a rabbet joint for the sides along with the dado for the bottom.

Materials

Bottom: ¾″ exterior plywood, B-C
one piece . . . . 29¼″ square

Sides: ¾″ pine, fir, or exterior plywood
two side pieces . . . . 9″ × 30″ (with ⅜″ rabbets)
two side pieces . . . . 9″ × 29¼″

Cut four sides from ¾-inch material—pine, fir, or plywood—and the bottom from ¾-inch plywood. Two sides are 29¼ inches long, while two others, the two to be rabbeted, are 30 inches long. The bottom is square to fit into the ⅜-inch deep dadoes (Illus. 5.8). The rabbets are cut ⅜ inch by ¾ inch to accept the ¾-inch side material (Illus. 5.9).

Assemble one of the sides without rabbets to the two sides with rabbets. Use one-inch brads and glue, and make sure the

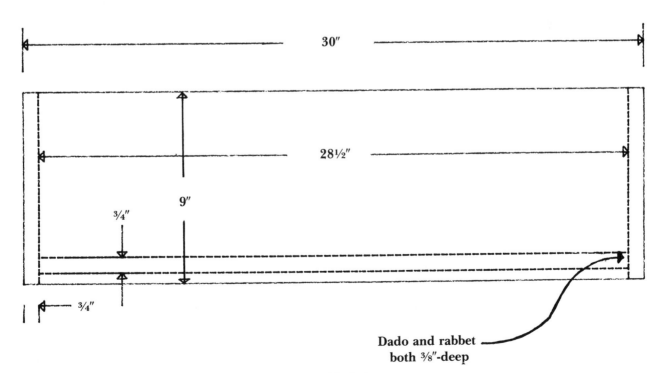

Illus. 5.7 Simple Sleeping Box using rabbet joints with dado.

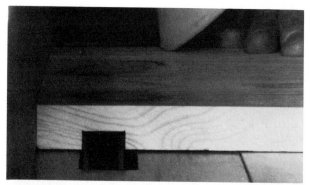

Illus. 5.8 Dado being cut.

Illus. 5.9 Cutting a rabbet. Note this box requires a wider rabbet.

corners are square. Then slip the bottom in the dado, and add the final side. Leave the bottom free floating. Glue and nail the last side in place. Check that the box is square, and set aside to allow the glue to dry.

Finish may be done with various stains. Use polyurethane over any stain for a protective coat.

Four Poster Dog Beds

These two beds really only differ in the height of the post, and number of frills turned into it (Illus. 5.10 and 5.11). The end and side boards are quite similar, and produced in the same manner. There are some further differences in the end and side boards, most noticeably the end boards of the second design are considerably wider. But you can easily size either design up or down. If you size up, it's also wise to increase the thickness of the posts to four inches, and the length of the side and head-board attachment block to six or eight inches, depending on the overall increase in size.

Longer Bedpost Style, Four Poster Dog Bed (Illus. 5.10). The plan for this dog bed is for small-to-medium-sized dogs. The plan can be simply changed to accommodate larger dogs by widening the head and foot boards and lengthening the side boards. Make changes in the posts, as mentioned above, according to the degree of alteration in size and your desires.

To begin constructing the longer bedpost style dog bed, turn four bedposts 22 inches tall, of 2⅜-inch square solid pine (Illus. 5.12). The attachment block is 4 inches long (Illus. 5.13), while the turned tape to the

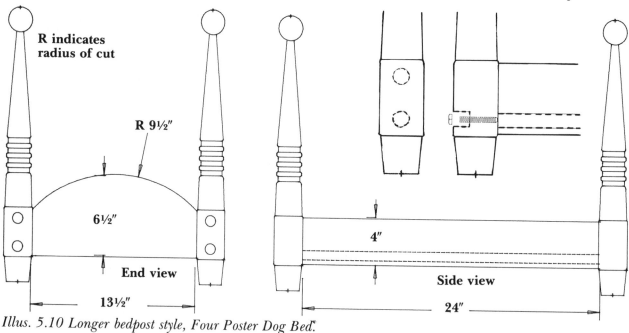

R indicates radius of cut

R 9½″

6½″

End view

13½″

4″

Side view

24″

Illus. 5.10 Longer bedpost style, Four Poster Dog Bed.

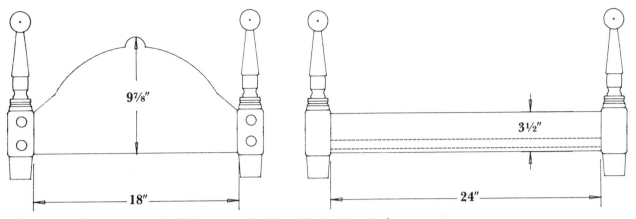

Illus. 5.11 Shorter cannonball bedpost style, Four Poster Dog Bed.

floor is 2 inches long, dropping from 2⅜ inch to 1⅞ inch (Illus. 5.14 and 5.15). This gives a short, fairly steep taper while assuring sufficient wood on the floor at each corner to make sure the bed doesn't wobble—and make the dog nervous, unable to rest.

Materials

Bedposts: solid pine lumber, 2⅜″ square
 make four, turned to finished length of 22″

Sides, ends:
 two side pieces, cut from one-by-six stock
 . . . . 24″ × 4″
 two end pieces . . . . 13½″ × 6½″

Bottom: ½″ or ¾″ exterior plywood, B-C
 cut to fit, side to side, end to end, notching corners for posts
 bottom support strips, use strips cut from one-by-six stock for sides

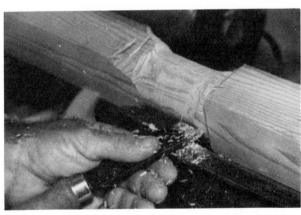

Illus. 5.13 Notch at top and bottom corners of attachment block to reduce chipping and splintering.

Illus. 5.14 Start removing material at the notches.

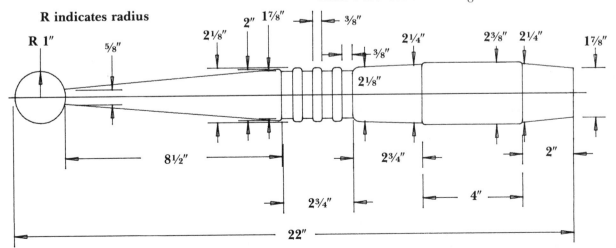

Illus. 5.12 Longer bedpost style pattern for turning.

Illus. 5.15 Continue removing waste until there is a round rod of the diameter of the largest pattern on that rod.

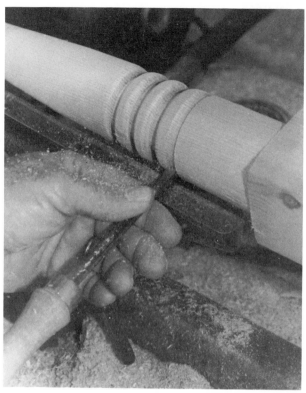

Illus. 5.17 Finishing turning the ring ornamentation.

The turning is capped with a 2-inch diameter ball on a ⅝-inch diameter neck that has tapered down from two inches over a distance of 8½ inches. Three rings offer decoration along the middle part of the bedpost (Illus. 5.16). The rings are ⅜-inch wide set on gaps of ⅜ inches (Illus. 5.17). The attachment block is cut to 2¼ inches at its top, and that round is tapered to 2⅛ inches before where the ⅜-inch depressed ring gap leading into the first ring is cut.

Once the first bedpost is cut, it is sanded (Illus. 5.18). This is most efficiently done with sanding strips, available in various widths beginning at one inch and in 50-yard lengths mounted on a cloth backing that is strong, but tears easily to allow for getting in narrow places. This first bedpost is most importantly used to mark the remaining bedposts (Illus. 5.19). Those are then turned and sanded.

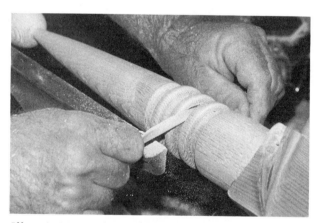

Illus. 5.18 Sanding the post.

Illus. 5.16 Starting to turn the rings.

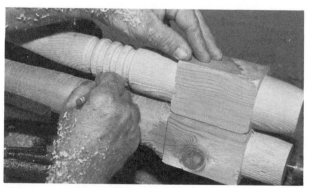

Illus. 5.19 Using the fully turned and sanded post to mark a partially turned post. This is the only way to transfer the pattern and ensure that all four finished posts will match.

When the posts are finished, the sides and ends are cut and formed. The ends in this design are 13½ inches wide and 6½ inches tall. The sides are 24 inches long and 4 inches wide cut from one-by-six stock—using the remaining "waste" strips to support the bottom, after being cut in half.

To get the arch in the ends, place two 6d finishing nails two inches down the sides, and one ¼ inch in from the edge at the middle. Thread a redwood slat of wood cut from an edge (use a slat ¼ inch thick by ¾ inch wide so it will bend easily), and use a pencil to outline the needed cuts (Illus. 5.20 and 5.21). This need be done only once, and the resulting piece, cut with a jigsaw or scroll saw, is used for a pattern.

Illus. 5.20 Use a redwood slat and nails to form the needed arch pattern.

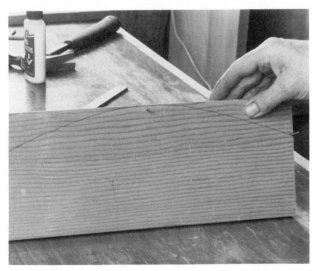

Illus. 5.21 When the pattern is drawn, all you need to do is pull the nails and cut. The cut piece can then serve as a pattern.

Install the bottom support strips with glue and 2d finishing nails along the bottom edge of the insides of the sides and the ends.

Now, drill for a ¼-inch dowel in one large (¾-inch or one-inch), flat-bottomed hole in the side attachment block. Drill two of these flat-bottomed holes, and drill a slightly smaller hole one inch deep in the lower hole. This will take a 2-inch by ¼-inch diameter lag screw (in the one-inch deep hole): the larger flat-bottomed hole leaves space for the lag screw to be turned in with a socket wrench.

Glue in the ¼-inch dowel—it makes no difference here whether the dowel is glued into the side or the side attachment block. Drill a mating hole in the side, and assemble the bed using clamps after applying glue to the unattached side of the dowel—the dowel may also be left dry on one side so that the bed can be disassembled. Make sure the assembly is square.

Now, install the lag screws. When the glue is dry, remove the clamps. Measure the inside from side to side and end to end, and cut a piece of plywood to size, notching the corners to fit around the attachment blocks. Drop the bottom piece in place, and cover with bedding or cedar shavings, as desired.

Shorter Cannonball Bedpost Style, Four Poster Dog Bed (Illus. 5.11). The plan for this dog bed is for medium-sized dogs. Alter the dimensions as needed to accommodate your dog. This design is broader than the first and thus looks closer to a scaled version of a cannonball bedpost bed. The bedposts themselves (Illus. 5.22) are somewhat shorter and differently decorated than those for the first four poster style dog bed.

The construction and assembly for this second style of four poster dog bed follows exactly that of the previous Longer Bedpost Style. To begin construction turn the four shorter bedposts, one at a time (Illus. 5.23, 5.24, and 5.25). Follow the bedpost pattern (Illus. 5.22) just as you did for the

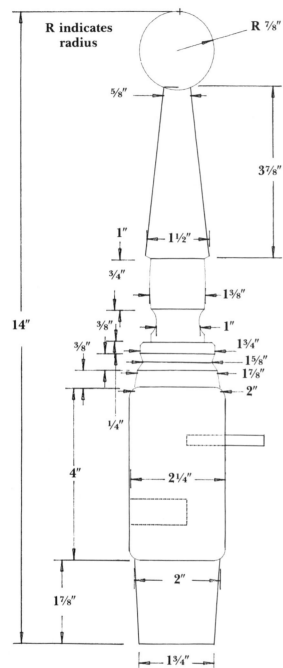

R indicates radius

R ⅞"

⅝"

3⅞"

1"

1½"

¾"

1⅜"

⅜"

1"

⅜"

1¾"

1⅝"

1⅞"

2"

14"

¼"

2¼"

4"

2"

1⅞"

1¾"

Illus. 5.22 Cannonball post pattern. Make four.

Illus. 5.23 Marking the attachment block: note the laminated fir used for this pattern.

Longer Bedpost Style. Here, the ball is 1¾ inches in diameter on a ⅝-inch neck (beware of a tendency of the ball to fly off during turning). The overall length is only 14 inches, again with a four-inch attachment block. The taper to the foot is over a length of 1⅞ inches, and the starting piece is 2¼ inches square (Illus. 5.26, 5.27, and 5.28).

Materials

Bedposts: glued-up fir or solid pine, cherry, walnut, poplar, maple
make four, turned to finished length of 14", 2¼" square

Sides, ends: solid lumber, as desired, to match posts
two side pieces . . . . 3¼" × 24"
two end pieces, arched . . . . 18" × 4" to
    9⅞" (overall)

Bottom: ½" or ¾" exterior plywood, B-C
cut to fit
bottom support strips . . . ¾" × ¾" × length as needed

Illus. 5.24 Notch attachment block corners.

Illus. 5.25 Turn the taper to the foot.

For this project I used glued-up fir to make the starting pieces for the posts. Fir turns with less tear out than does solid pine. Most hardwoods, such as cherry, walnut, poplar, and maple, also turn with less tear out, and are easier to finish, assuming you have sharp tools. The taper for the section into the cannonball starts at 5⅝ inches from the top, and is 3⅞ inches long (Illus. 5.29 and 5.30). Once you have completed the first post, sand it (Illus. 5.31), and use it to mark the others (Illus. 5.32).

Illus. 5.26 Use calipers to check on proper ball diameter.

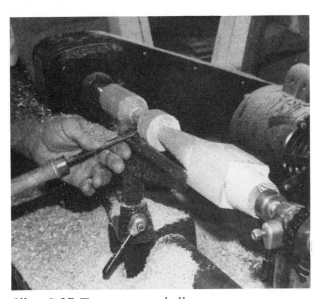

Illus. 5.27 Turn taper to ball.

Illus. 5.28 Size ball to marks.

Illus. 5.29 Taper to ball.

Illus. 5.30 Round off the ball.

Illus. 5.31 Sand.

Illus. 5.32 Mark the next block for turning.

End height is 9⅞ inches, and the ends may have a blip to that height or simply be smoothly arched as was the case for the ends for the previous four poster style. The end width is 18 inches, and the height tapers down to four inches, just as with the other style.

The side is 3¼ inches by 24 inches long. A ¾-inch square strip is attached along the sides and ends, just as you did for the first style. These will hold the bottom piece.

The bottom is cut from ½-inch or ¾-inch B-C exterior plywood, used B side up, and set in on the strips. Assembly of the bed posts, sides, and ends is done exactly as in the preceding design.

For both designs, if your dog is a restless type, you may want to use one or two 2d finishing nails on each side to hold the bottom securely in place.

6
Cat Homes and Projects

Feline home projects present some different, if not more, problems than do doghouse projects. Their origins aren't difficult to ascertain: fewer people seem interested in housing cats outdoors, and fewer cats seem interested in what we might describe as formal housing.

The relationships are about the same—with the larger houses being suitable for larger cats and smaller ones for smaller cats—but there is generally less variation in the size of domestic cats than dogs. While the size variation for all felines, feral included, is greater than for canines, the difference among ordinary domestic cats is small enough to not require any great variations in sizes for homes and toys, or accessory items.

Cats also prefer a secure feeling—the chance of curling up knowing nothing is going to get too close to them. That tendency makes an outdoor home less likely to serve for occupation unless the cat is only an outdoor cat.

My suggestion, formed by watching a long line of cats take over my various homes in the past several decades, is a simple one:

build a house that is large enough to hold all your cats at one time, even if they have to stack themselves to get in (they usually will). Then site the house on a corner of a deck railing or a similar spot that is easily reached by the cat—and less easily reached by other animals. A height of between two and three feet above the surface seems to serve well.

Two-Storey Cat Quarters

This is a good sized home, meant for several cats at one time (Illus. 6.1). With the two-storey country-house look—complete with a front porch and balcony—this house makes a very handsome, yet basically simple, project to provide "living quarters" for your cat(s).

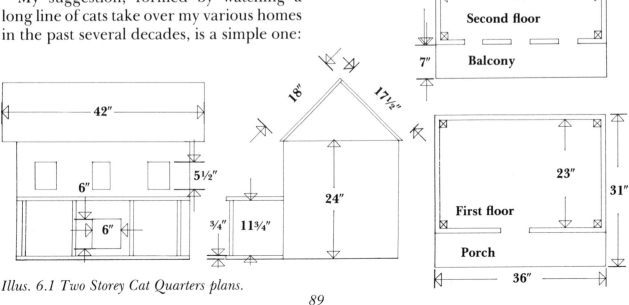

Illus. 6.1 Two Storey Cat Quarters plans.

Materials

Floors: ¾" exterior plywood, B-C

first floor piece . . . . 36" × 31"

second floor piece, cut in several stages . . . . . .
starting piece is 36" × 30½", then in 7" (balcony) reduce width to 35" by removing ½" strips from both edges, 23½" long

Roof, walls: ½" exterior plywood or stock

one of two roof pieces . . . . 42" × 17½"
(or 19½" for overhang)

second of two roof pieces . . . . 42" × 18"
(or 20" for overhang)

two end walls . . . . 24" × 23"

gables, cut to fit for outdoor use only rear wall piece . . . . 24" × 36"

two front wall pieces . . . . 11¼" × 36"

Corner and porch supports:

eight two-by-two corner supports . . . .
11¼" lengths

four ¾"-dowel balcony supports . . . .
11¼" lengths

Start by cutting the eight two-by-two corner floor supports and wall braces along with the four ¾-inch dowel balcony supports, all to a length of 11¼ inches. Cut the two front wall pieces 36 inches long and both also 11¼ inches high. Cut the rear wall piece 24 inches high by 36 inches long. Cut the two end walls 24 inches by 23 inches. Leave the gable ends open for indoor use, or close with a separate piece after the rest of the house is fully assembled, measuring and cutting to fit to ensure accuracy, if the house is for the outdoors.

Cut the first floor piece a full 31 inches deep by 36 inches wide, and start cutting the second floor piece by first cutting a simple piece 30½ inches deep by 36 inches wide. The second floor piece has to fit inside the rear and end walls but still be full width along the balcony to match the porch floor below. Measure 7 inches in and mark a reduced width from the full 36 inches to 35 inches by marking off ½-inch wide strips for the remaining 23½-inch depth.

Cut the two roof pieces so that they overlap at the peak, and increase the width if you desire more overhang, front and back.

Both pieces are 42 inches wide, and one is either 17½ inches or 19½ inches high, while the second is either 18 inches or 20 inches high, respectively, according to your preference for the overhang.

To prepare for assembly, cut the second floor back corners to allow a cat to easily get from one floor to the next. I suggest using a radius of about 5½ inches with the corners lopped starting about 4 inches in from each corner as shown (Illus. 6.1, second floor view). The two front wall pieces should also be cut; one with the door in the middle, and the other with three 3-inch by 5½-inch high windows placed as you choose, but making sure they are at least two inches in from each corner to clear the corner wall braces.

Begin assembly by gluing and nailing the back wall on top of the first floor piece, flush to the rear. Next attach the two end walls, which will fit inside both the front and rear walls. Install the lower front wall—with the door opening—and glue and nail the inside corner supports.

Place the upper front wall piece and attach the corner wall braces. The balcony should be 36 inches wide and 7 inches deep, matching the porch below, now that all the pieces are assembled. Support the front edge of the balcony with the four 11¼-inch lengths of ¾-inch dowel, nailed and glued top and bottom.

Attach the two roof pieces, front overlapping back. If you plan to use this house outdoors, or if you simply prefer, measure and install ½-inch thick plywood triangles for the gable ends.

Finish your new Two-Storey Cat Quarters as you wish, for indoor or outdoor use.

Cat Abode

This simple Cat Abode goes together in a hurry, yet allows all sorts of decorative touches because it is so easy and quick to assemble. The basic seven pieces can be cut from less than half a sheet of ½-inch exterior plywood (Illus. 6.2). You can increase the roof lengths to allow for an overhang at

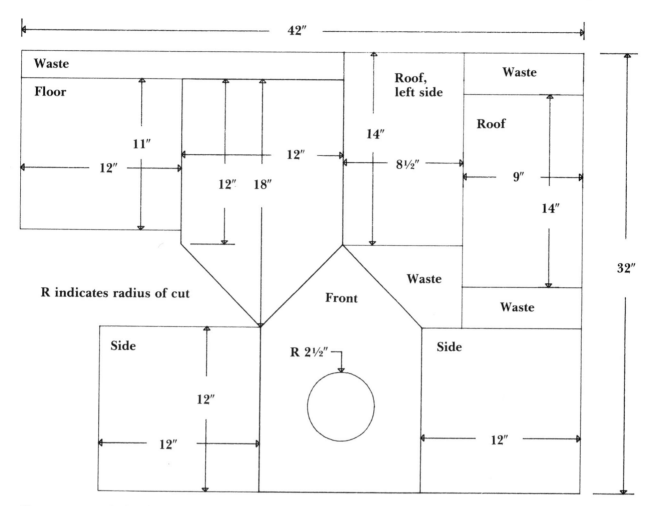

Illus. 6.2 Cat Abode plan.

the eaves, or provide the overhang by shingling—as the project is designed. Decorative variations include changes in shingle style, entry location, or color choices, and the addition of various kinds of trim, including some types of gingerbread available at local woodworking dealers and by mail. The basic Cat Abode can thus become almost any style you desire.

Allowing for ⅛-inch kerfs, cut the pieces as shown (Illus. 6.2). As you'll note, the entry hole in the front was cut using a "fly cutter" (Illus. 6.3 and 6.4). The drill and circle cutter do a neat job, but under normal shop circumstances, this is most safely done on a drill press. I used a heavy-duty ½-inch variable-speed hand-held drill and experienced nothing I would consider to be danger with this type of circle cutter, but with some versions there is excessive danger using hand equipment. I recommend that you stick to the drill press. In all hon-

Illus. 6.3 Setting up to cut the entry hole: note the weight of the variable speed drill to be used, and the fact that it has its side handle in place.

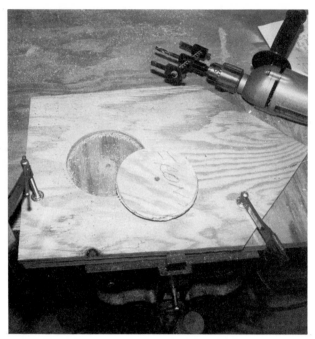

Illus. 6.4 Finishing cutting the entry hole.

esty, this setup provided all the pounding my elbows and forearms were likely to need for the following six months. The cutter has a strong tendency to grab and try to jerk the drill out of your hands. If you do use a hand-held setup, be *very careful* and make absolutely sure that the piece being cut is firmly clamped: worrying about the cutter flying apart is enough!

Cutting the pieces and assembly are fairly simple, so that you can easily make any variations in the design that you desire. The house is actually large enough for more than one cat, and positioning the entry hole about 6 inches up the front makes it quite suitable for most cats. If you have an expectant mother cat, you might want to increase the entry to a 6-inch or even an 8-inch hole. Such large holes will have to be cut using a jigsaw.

Assemble the floor piece inside the front piece and a side piece (Illus. 6.5). Place the opposite side piece and the back piece in place, and attach with the 2d galvanized nails. With correct assembly, the side pieces butt directly up against the front and back pieces, and the floor piece is entirely surrounded by the four walls (Illus. 6.6). Assemble the roof pieces so that there will be an overlap at the ridge (Illus. 6.7).

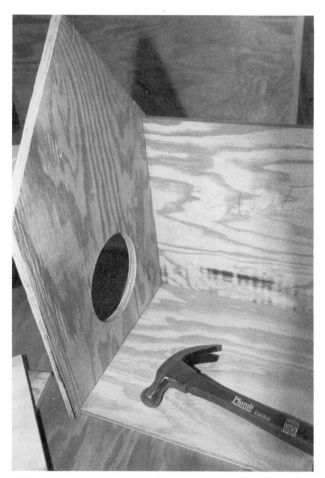

Illus. 6.5 Wall assembly begun.

Illus. 6.6 Basic assembly completed.

The basic Cat Abode is completely assembled and ready to have any roof covering or decorative trim applied and painted, as desired (Illus. 6.8).

Illus. 6.7 Adding the roof pieces.

Illus. 6.8 The basic cat abode, assembled, but unfinished.

New England Salt Box Feline Fun House

Rather than merely provide practical housing, this basic design is meant to encourage cats to play, alone and with each other (Illus. 6.9). Though the house looks like it has two storeys, it actually has only the one. If you do want a working second floor, then add at least six inches to the height. The windows are small, half painted and half cut out. Instead of painting, you can use narrow wood strips as trim. The windows

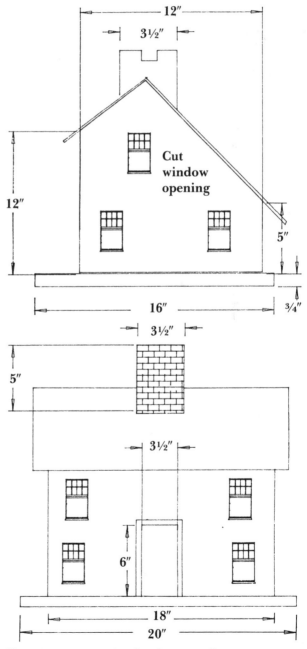

Illus. 6.9 New England Salt Box Feline Fun House plans.

are 2¾ inches high by 1½ inches wide. You can change the size as they are only big enough to allow a paw to exit, though cats love poking paws through holes. This is the main reason for cutting out the windows rather than painting them in entirely or leaving the sides and front blank. However, if you intend to use the house as practical housing, then don't cut out the windows, and use paint, trim, or leave them blank instead. The chimney is also optional.

Materials

Base: ¾" exterior plywood
floor piece . . . . 20" × 16"

Roof, walls: ½" exterior plywood
one of two roof pieces . . . . 20" × 9"
second of two roof pieces . . . . 20" × 16"
front wall piece . . . . 18" × 12" (15°
   bevel on top edge)
back wall piece . . . . 18" × 5" (30°
   bevel on top edge)
two end walls . . . . 12" × 15" (at peak)
   (end walls are 12" at the front and 5" at the
   back)

Chimney (optional): ½" plywood or solid wood,
3½" square

Door trim: ½" × ⅜" stock, cut to fit

Cut the pieces as indicated above. The 2¾-inch high by 1½-inch wide windows have openings about 1½-inches square cut in them. As noted this allows the cats to play but not get through the windows. To make the house suitable for outdoor use, eliminate the openings for windows and add a shingled exterior after the house is assembled. Cut the 6-inch by 3½-inch door in the front piece, and trim this opening with the ½-inch by ⅜-inch stock, using epoxy to secure the pieces.

Assemble the house with the sides inside the front and back. Position the assembled unit, after making sure it is square, on the base, applying epoxy as a start. Either turn the house over, and drive 2d finishing nails to secure the assembly, or leave everything upright and attach corner braces inside the house to make sure the base and the walls stay fastened together.

Finally, put on the roof, making sure the pieces overlap, back over front. If you choose to include the chimney, cut an angled notch in it to fit the roof.

If the house is to be used out of doors, shingle with cedar shim stock and seal it with a good quality water repellent. Finish with an opaque stain in a suitably "New England" color—dark grey, dark red, etc., with white trim.

Cat Play River Steamboat

Toys for cats are possibly more rewarding to build than are houses. Cats play more than almost any other animals—except, perhaps, otters—and are a great deal of fun to watch. Making them a toy such as this Cat Play River Steamboat (Illus. 6.10) that allows them to slink, crawl, and finally relax on or about it, can provide hours of fun, for feline and human companion alike.

Materials

Base: two-by-twelve lumber, redwood, pine, fir, etc.
one piece . . . . 26" length, front radius 5¼"

Top deck: two-by-ten lumber, redwood, pine, fir, etc.
one piece . . . . 21½" length, radius 4⅛"

Texas roof: one-by-eight lumber, redwood, pine, fir, etc.
one piece . . . . 7½" length, radius 3"

Paddlewheel:
two plywood circles . . . . 8" diameter
two angled one-by-three pieces . . . . 14"
   length, radius 1⅛"
four lathe strips . . . . cut to fit
middle dowel piece . . . . cut to fit

Smokestacks: two turned pieces

Deck supports: 1"-diameter dowel
six pieces (set into ½" holes, above and below)
. . . . .8¼" lengths
four railings of ¼" dowel . . . . cut to fit

Roof supports: ½"-diameter dowel
four pieces (set into ½" holes, above and below)
. . . . 6" lengths

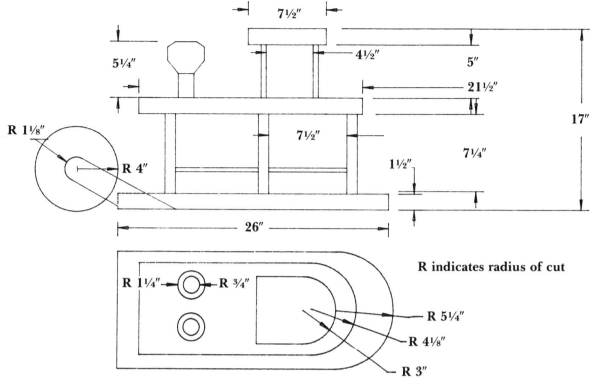

Illus. 6.10 Cat Play River Steamboat plan.

Start construction by cutting the base. Redwood scraps from building a deck are really ideal, but almost any solid wood will be fine. Cut the boat's top deck piece and the Texas roof piece as well. Be sure to plan ahead on making the semicircular cuts that define the front end for each piece. These should produce a similar look for each of the different width pieces: the base is cut with a 5¼-inch radius, the deck with a 4⅛-inch radius, and the roof with a 3-inch radius. Make sure to slightly round or bevel the edges of these pieces to help prevent splinters.

Cut the deck supports from the one-inch dowel to 8¼-inch lengths, to set into ½-inch holes in the base and the bottom of the upper deck. Join the dowels as shown (Illus. 6.11) about two inches up from the bottom deck, with ¼-inch diameter dowels to serve

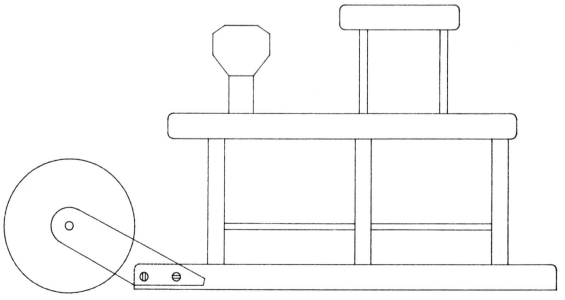

Illus. 6.11 Side view detail of Steamboat. Note rounded edges to prevent splinters.

as railings. Use ½-inch diameter dowels to support the Texas roof, with the dowels 6 inches long, set into ½-inch deep holes.

Keep in mind that most of the dimensions can be varied depending on your materials and inclination, but the really critical sizes are the support heights that let cats slink through the decks. Use the dimensions given on the plan as a guide to turning two pieces for the smokestacks. Drill holes for the two smokestacks, and glue the turned smokestack pieces in place.

Cut two 8-inch diameter circles on a band saw. Cut a piece of 14-inch long one-by-three with a radius of 1⅛ inch at one end, and angled to the fit at the other. Fit the 8-inch circles onto the rounded end of the pieces, using a dowel through the middle. The 8-inch circles are joined with four lathe strips nailed around the perimeter with 2d finishing nails. This forms the "paddle-wheel" for the steamboat. Screw or nail the angled pieces to the base so that the 8-inch circles just clear the base and the floor.

Finish with your own combination of colors: redwood deserves to be left clear, while the colors applied to the hardwood dowels and smokestacks can provide contrast. The plywood parts should be painted as desired.

Cat Play Box

This play box is simple to construct, and the top pattern does not have to be followed exactly (Illus. 6.12). Its use is also simple. It has no bottom, and so it is just placed over a catnip mouse, ball, or other cat toy, and the cat is then allowed to play with the toy through the slots in the box, usually trying to get it out.

Start by cutting the 2¼-inch side pieces from ½-inch plywood or other scrap stock. Cut two at 18 inches and two at 17 inches. Assemble the shorter set inside the longer pieces using glue and 2d nails.

Cut an 18-inch square from the ¾-inch plywood for the top. Use a jigsaw and a drill to cut the patterns as shown (Illus. 6.12). The five circles are 2 inches in diameter.

The middle slots are cut at either end with a ¾-inch radius, and the corner slot patterns have a ½-inch radius. These dimensions are not critical: vary the pattern design and measurements in any way that appeals to you.

Finish the Cat Play Box by decorating it with bright enamel paint. And don't forget to supply a toy or two for your cat—a catnip-filled or -soaked ball works very well.

Materials

Top: ¾″ plywood, B-C
 one piece . . . . 18″ square
 slot pattern, middle . . . . 4¼″ × ¾″ radius
 slot pattern, corner . . . . 4½″ × ½″ radius
 circle patterns, five . . . . 1″ radius
 (2″ from edge and at middle)

Sides: ½″ plywood or other scrap stock
 two pieces . . . . 2¼″ × 18″
 two pieces . . . . 2¼″ × 17″

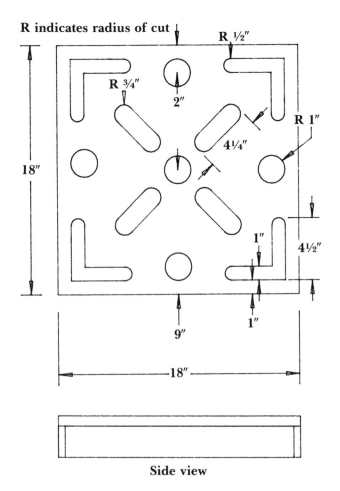

Illus. 6.12 Cat Play Box plan.

Cat Play Pickup Truck

This is a cat play vehicle that can be made to roll or to just stay put (Illus. 6.13). In either case, this toy is meant for cats to sit on, play with, roll around and over, and to get their other toys like catnip mice and balls stuck under to be fished out with a long arm and paw—with claw perhaps. The toy requires all solid wood construction, except perhaps the wheels, which can be commercial models—wood or other material.

The cab is assembled from solid stock, glued up from six pieces of two-by-six lumber in combination with a one-by-six piece to yield a full 10-inch width. The width is to provide play room for the cats, so that you may ignore the exact width given and decide to just use the six pieces without the one-by-six odd size, or produce a slightly wider pickup by using seven pieces of two-by-six. But be sure to take your decision into consideration when you build the pickup bed and cut the axles. In any case, use pieces that will be 10¼ inches after trimming and finishing.

Materials

Truck cab: two-by-six and one-by-six (if desired) stock
six or seven two-by-six pieces . . . . 10¼"
  finished length
a one-by-six piece (as required) . . . . 10¼"
  finished length

Pickup bed:
base of ¾"-thick lumber . . . . 8½" × 9¾"
two side pieces, two-by-four . . . . 9¾" × 3"
  (cut down)

Truck tires: commercial or homemade
four wheels . . . . 2⅝" diameter
two axles, dowel pieces or commercial

The cab is cut with the entry door-shaped as shown (Illus. 6.13), which may be cut individually in each piece before being glued up, or the cab can be assembled in halves, allowing sufficient clearance for most band saws. The full 10-inch width is too much to cut all at once on the band saw. Assembling the cab in halves also allows you to do any other shaping and smoothing then, before the two pieces are glued up.

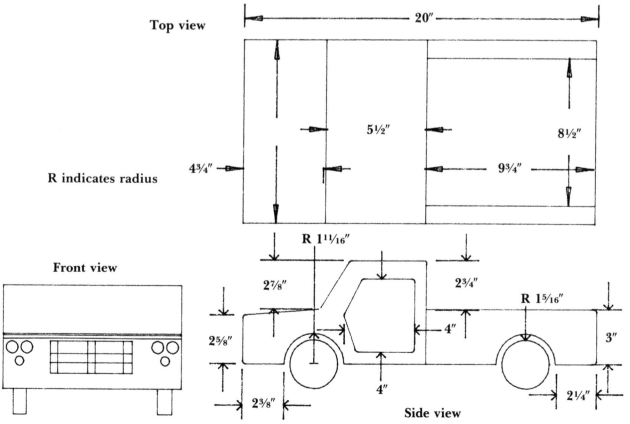

Illus. 6.13 Cat Play Pickup Truck plans.

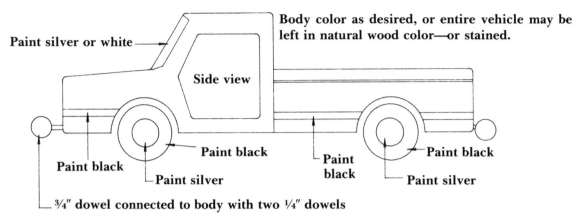

Paint silver or white

Side view

Body color as desired, or entire vehicle may be left in natural wood color—or stained.

Paint black

Paint silver

Paint black

Paint black

Paint black

Paint silver

¾″ dowel connected to body with two ¼″ dowels

Illus. 6.14 Cat Play Pickup, side view optional finishing detail.

The windshield angle and hood, for instance, should be cut before the cab is assembled. The wheel wells don't require such a deep cutting clearance, so they can be cut at any time. Do the final smoothing, of course, after the cab is fully assembled.

The pickup bed has no back or front. The two sides are two-by-four cut down to a width of three inches. The base of the bed matches the length of the sides at 9¾ inches, is ¾ inch thick by 8½ inches wide, and is glued and nailed inside the two side pieces. Cut the wheel well openings at a 3⅝-inch diameter before the sides are assembled to the base.

Use 2⅝″ commercial wheels (or other size, as you desire). Adjust the wheel wells to both the front and the back to suit the wheels you choose. The commercial wheels will take short axles, or you can use your own dowel pieces.

Paint, or stain, as desired and depending on materials used (Illus. 6.14). If the pickup truck is stained, put on several coats of clear polyurethane.

Bumpers are optional, as is the suggested paint scheme.

Scratch Pad

Cats as we all know are forever scratching at things. This is an essential part of their nature, more commonly seen in indoor cats than outdoor: the cats scratch both to help shed their nail husks, keeping their nails sharp and short enough to be sheathed, as well as to simply stretch and exercise their forearm muscles—the behavior is still present in cats that have been long since declawed. If we provide them with something to exercise on, it may save on furniture and drapes (Illus. 6.15).

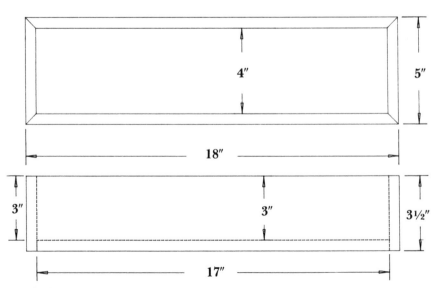

4″   5″

18″

3″   3″   3½″

17″

Illus. 6.15 Scratch Pad plan.

Materials

Box base, sides, ends: ½″ stock or ¾″ stock, as desired
(use planed one-by-four solid pine, fir, etc., or plywood)
one base piece . . . . 17″ × 4″ (or 16½″ × 3½″ for ¾″)
two side pieces . . . . 18″ × 3½″ depth
two end pieces . . . . 5″ × 3½″ (mitred), 4″ × 3½″ (butt)

Removable inner piece:
two-by-four ripped to 3″ width, cut to fit

Inner piece covering: carpet scrap

This is a simple box, though the corners have been mitred on the plan for a neat look. The box is made from solid one-by-four stock, pine, fir or other wood that's on hand. You can also decide to use ½-inch plywood. The stock is planed to ½ inch thickness. Cut a base piece 4 inches by 17 inches (if you would rather use ¾-inch thick stock, decrease the inside width to 3½ inches by a 16½ inch length). Cut two sides 18 inches by 3½ inches. Cut two ends 5 inches by 3½ inches. If you don't wish to mitre the corners, then cut the ends 4 inches by 3½ inches, and set them inside to form a butt joint with the sides.

Finish the box with stain and clear finish.

Now, cut a piece of two-by-four for the inner scratching piece, and rip it to 3 inches wide. Wrap this inner piece in carpet, stapled in place. Sprinkle the carpet with catnip. The carpet will provide an excellent cat exerciser, and the box should help keep the catnip off the floor.

Cat Playhouse

This plywood playhouse goes together quickly, and will provide cats with hours of fun, and owners with hours of enjoyment watching their pets (Illus. 6.16). This is a roofless version meant for indoor use, but you can easily add a roof.

Cut the floor, front and back each 18 inches square. Cut the sides 11 inches by 18 inches and the second floor 17 inches by 11 inches. The porch roof is cut 6¼ inches deep by 18 inches long and is supported by 9 inch long ½-inch diameter dowels set into ¼-inch deep holes in the porch floor and roof.

The porch roof sits on a ½-inch by 18-inch wide strip that has a 10° bevel on its house side where it is attached.

Windows, doors, and portholes are cut as shown, and the patterns may be changed, if desired. Round all the corners for windows and doors. No cutouts are shown for the

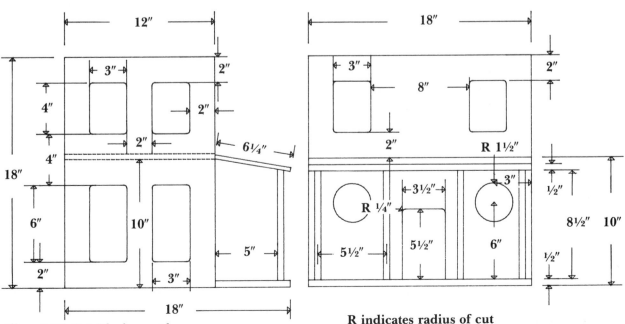

Illus. 6.16 Cat Playhouse plans.

R indicates radius of cut

back wall, but sizes similar to those used in the side walls are recommended if cutouts are desired all around. Do not forget to make a cutout of about 4 inches by 6 inches in one corner of the second floor to allow the cats easy passage to and from the first floor.

Materials

Floor, porch roof, sides, front, back, second floor: ½″ plywood
one floor piece . . . . 18″ × 18″
one porch roof piece . . . . 18″ × 6¼″
two side pieces . . . . 18″ × 11″
front and back pieces . . . . 18″ × 18″
second floor piece . . . . 17″ × 11″

Porch supports: ½″-diameter dowel pieces and scrap lumber
four pieces set in ¼″-deep holes . . . . 9″ lengths
roof support strip . . . . ½″ × 18″ cut from scrap

Main roof (optional): ½″ plywood
set-in roof (same as second floor) . . . 17″ × 11″
outdoor overhanging roof . . . . 20″ × 14″

Assembly is fast and the playhouse may be readily increased for larger cats: be sure to enlarge all of the windows, doors, and portholes as well.

The second floor is set in with glue and 4d finishing nails. Otherwise, the house is assembled with glue and 2d finishing nails, sanded, and painted as desired.

There is no roof needed for this playhouse since it is meant to be used indoors by one or more cats or kittens. If you prefer a roof, set one in, making it the same size as the second floor. For outdoor use, make the roof larger so that it sits on top of the walls and overhangs.

Cat Play Stairs

This set of play stairs provides cats with exercise and fun (Illus. 6.17). The openings may be varied in their shape, size, or location, but this configuration seems to work pretty well.

Start by cutting the two side stair treads 12 inches wide by 7 inches deep. Next, cut the top tread 12 inches wide by 8 inches deep.

Cut the two sides, starting with a piece that is 18 inches by 12 inches. Then cut out 6-inch by 6-inch corner pieces for the stairway on each side of the top stair position.

Drill or cut the holes either as marked or in your own design. Assemble with no stair overhang at the sides, using 4d nails and glue.

Finish the Cat Play Stairs by painting as desired.

Materials

Stair treads, sides: ¾″ plywood, B-C
top stair tread . . . . 12″ × 8″
two side stair treads . . . . 12″ × 7″
two side pieces . . . . 18″ × 12″ (overall, with 6″ × 6″ corners cut out for side treads)

Bottom and top stair end risers (optional): ¾″ plywood, B-C
four riser pieces . . . . 10½″ × 6″

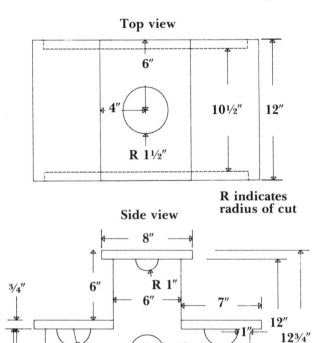

Illus. 6.17 Cat Play Stairs plan.

If you wish, you can increase the hiding possibilities of the play stairs by simply cutting and installing risers. Cut four 6-inch tall by 10½-inch wide pieces, and nail them in the riser positions, with or without holes cut in them. At least one 3-inch diameter hole in the middle of each of the bottom risers would be best.

Two-Storey Cat Silo

This octagonal silo works as a playhouse, or as an actual house (Illus. 6.18).

Materials

Floor, roof, sides: ½″ stock, solid or plywood, as desired

one first floor piece .... 11″ × 11″ (octagonal, 135°)

one roof piece .... 11″ × 11″ (octagonal, 135°)

four side pieces .... 24″ × 5″ (square ends)

four mitred side pieces .... 24″ × 5″ (45°, outside dimensions)

Start construction by cutting eight pieces 5 inches wide by 24 inches long from ½-inch stock. These are for the sides of the octagon, but four will be left as is with square-cut ends while the other four should be mitred on either side at a 45° angle.

The mitred and the unmitred pieces are the same thickness, however when the mitred cut is placed up against the square-edged sides with the outer surfaces flush, you will find that the mitred surface is wider. This means that the mitred piece actually juts in towards the interior of the octagon, which is not shown exactly in Illus. 6.18. Take this into account when you lay out the roof and floor pieces. There may just be a slight gap near each side joint: the roof and floor are cut 11 inches by 11 inches with a 135° angle at each of the eight corners.

The inner floor level is set up 12 inches. Cut either a 4-inch diameter rounded hole or a 3-inch by 4-inch rectangular hole in the floor to allow the cats access for play and to move about freely.

The arched door is 3-inches wide and 5½-inches high, with the arch cut on a 1½-inch radius. There is a 2½-inch to 3-inch diameter window set in the second storey. You may repeat the window, or other cutout designs, at various spots around the octagonal silo, as desired.

Finish or paint the completed cat silo according to the wood used and your desires.

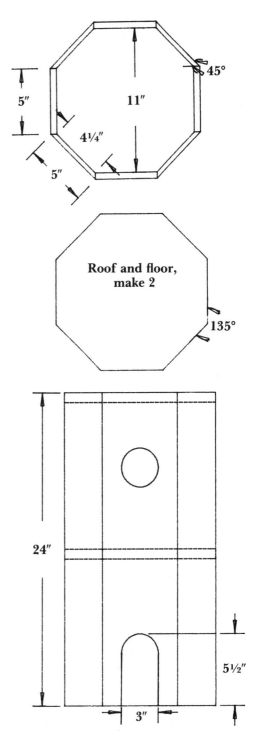

Illus. 6.18 Two-Storey Cat Silo plans.

Cat Sleeping Box

This finger-jointed cat sleeping box, especially when done in top grade woods such as maple and walnut as the one I made was, can add a touch of elegance and natural beauty to your cat's daily life without requiring a complicated assembly or finishing job on your part (Illus. 6.19). While maple and walnut are desirable, this sleeping box may just as readily be done in pine, or fir.

Materials

Sides: ¾″ maple and walnut preferable, or pine, fir, etc.
three sides . . . . 12″ × 5½″
front side, with 1½″-deep cutout . . . 12″ × 5½″

Bottom: ¼″ poplar plywood
one piece to fit in dadoes . . . . . . 12¾″ × 12¾″

To begin construction, I suggest selecting one length of one-by-six material and cutting the bottom-edge dado first. If you want the natural contrast for the finger joints, then use two woods such as the maple and walnut I used, and cut the dadoes into lengths of each from which to cut the separate sides. Cut the dado ⅜ inch up from the bottom, ¼ inch wide by ⅜ inch deep. Then cut the dadoed piece or pieces into

one foot lengths: all four sides are the same size, but make the cutout only in the front side as shown (Illus. 6.19).

Cut the ⅜-inch finger joints on your table saw (Illus. 6.20). Use a shopmade jig like the one I described earlier (page 27) or a commercial model.

Cut the bottom piece from the ¼-inch plywood 12¾ inches square to allow for the fit into the dadoes (Illus. 6.21).

Illus. 6.20 Cutting finger joints for the Cat Sleeping Box, in a walnut side.

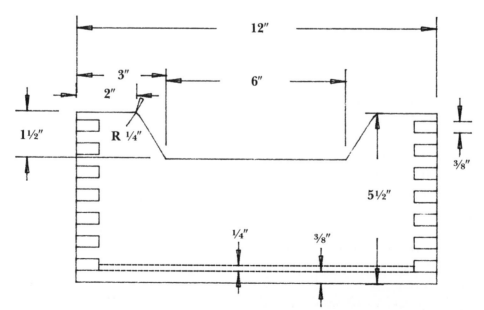

Illus. 6.19 Cat Sleeping Box plan.

Illus. 6.21 Parts ready for assembly.

Start assembling the sleeping box by joining two sides (Illus. 6.22), after which the bottom piece is slipped into the dadoes. While all the finger joints should be carefully glued, do **NOT** glue the bottom in place. Apply glue for the other two sides, and assemble all of the finger joints, checking for square. The bottom piece is supported by the dadoes and locked in place by the finger joints.

If you have made the sleeping box as I did, of top-grade woods, simply sand and finish (Illus. 6.23). If you've used pine or fir, you might want to use a stain before applying a clear wood finish.

Illus. 6.22 Assembled corner.

Illus. 6.23 Preparing to finish the sleeping box.

Pencil Post Cat Bed

With turned posts for dog beds, I didn't want to let cats go without fancy sleeping accessories. Thus, this bed with its tapered posts, and arched footboard and headboard seemed just right (Illus. 6.24).

Materials

Bottom: ½″ plywood
   one piece . . . . 12¼″ × 24″

Sides: one-by-four pieces
   two side pieces . . . . 3½″ × 24″
   two bottom support strips . . . . ¾″ × 1
      × 24″

End boards: one-by-seven material
   one arched headboard piece . . . . 12¼″ × 7″
      (at peak)
   one arched footboard piece . . . . 12¼″ × 7″
      or lower (as desired)

Pencil posts: 2″ square pieces of fir
   four posts, 4″ base, tapering to ¾″ square top

Top post supports (optional): one-by-one material
   four ¾″-square pieces: cut and notched to fit

Start by cutting 2-inch square pieces of fir, 16 inches long. Mark up from the bottom of each piece 4 inches to define the base of each leg. Place two layers of masking tape at the lines drawn on all four sides.

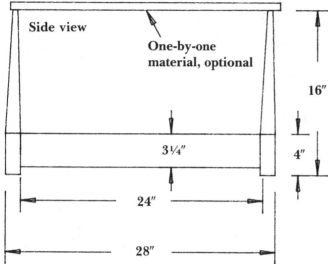

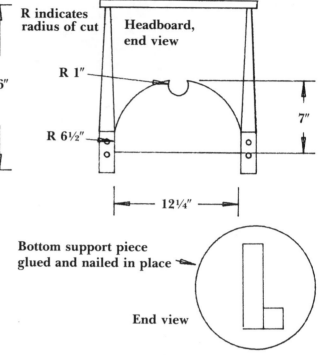

Illus. 6.24 Pencil Post Cat Bed plan.

The masking tape is needed because otherwise the machine used to create the taper will snipe, or nip out too much of, the material at the marked line (Illus. 6.25).

Set your jointer on 1/16 inch or 1/8 inch. My Ryobi jointer will not take a full 1/8-inch cut, so I used the 1/16-inch setting and twice as many passes. The cut starts at the taped mark, where the post is lowered onto the spinning blades (Illus. 6.25). *You must use care here,* for the guard has to be held back, and your hands are going to be closer than is really sensible to sharp, spinning metal blades. Once the blades bite, use a push block (Illus. 6.26). After you get the taper started, *you must use a push block,* because the ends taper down, bringing your fingers much too close to the blades (Illus. 6.27).

Illus. 6.26 Use push blocks as cut moves along.

Illus. 6.25 Starting a taper cut. Note that the guard is drawn back, and held out of the way. **BE CAREFUL!**

Illus. 6.27 The push block is even more important as you do the last few cuts and your fingers get closer to the blades.

Taper all four legs to match, with the tapered end being ¾-inch square. Start by making one cut on one side, then make the next cut on the next side. Go on around the post until the taper is completed, using the same pattern—if you vary it, you'll lose track, and the taper will be off one or more cuts to one side or another.

Once the posts are made, I recommend that you go ahead and cut the top supports. These pieces are strictly optional, but they will strengthen the cat bed and render the spiky posts harmless in case you have small children in the house. These are of one-by-one material (thus, ¾-inch square). Notch each end where it fits over the post so that you get a half-lap joint in the supports (Illus. 6.24). Measure for the supports individually, before notching: that is, set the cut pieces aside while you assemble the headboard, footboard, and sides, before making the final notch cuts to fit the supports.

Cut sides 24 inches long, of 3½-inch wide stock. Lay in a ¾-inch by 1-inch support for the bottom on each side (see detail, Illus. 6.24). Cut the ends from the one-by-seven material, and cut a 6½-inch radius arch from end to end in thé 12¼-inch wide headboard piece. The footboard can be a much lower, gradual arch, as desired. Use the same technique illustrated for the end boards of the dog beds (Illus. 5.20 and 5.21, page 85). Place a wood slat arched under two end nails and over a middle nail set at the top of the end board.

If desired, cut a 1-inch radius circle off center for a decorative flourish to the headboard as shown in Illus. 6.24.

Assemble using dowels into the end boards (Illus. 6.28), and lag screws into the side boards (this allows the bed to be taken apart and carried elsewhere).

The bottom is ½-inch plywood, cut 12¼ inches by 24 inches, with the corners notched to fit around the posts.

Finish your Pencil Post Cat Bed, staining as desired or protecting the wood with only a clear finish. Provide some soft bedding and your cat will probably move right in for a nap.

Illus. 6.28 Assembled footboard.

Cat Carrier

Getting cats from one place to another is simple for some, not so simple for others. One very relaxed cat would sleep against the back of my neck on the driver's seat, while others would go wild and even get sick once placed in a vehicle. A Maine coon cat that I had started moaning and frothing the instant the engine was started, and didn't stop even on very long trips. Tranquilizing cats is not always a good idea and carries risks, so I would rather put up with the peccadilloes—but this can be made safer, and perhaps more pleasant for all, if the cats are enclosed.

When transport for long distances and times is needed, a good cat carrier is virtually indispensable. You can ensure that the animal arrives safely and in good shape. As well, if the cat has been allowed to sleep in the carrier at other times, when not travelling, the cat may actually be quite content being in the familiar and secure space. This

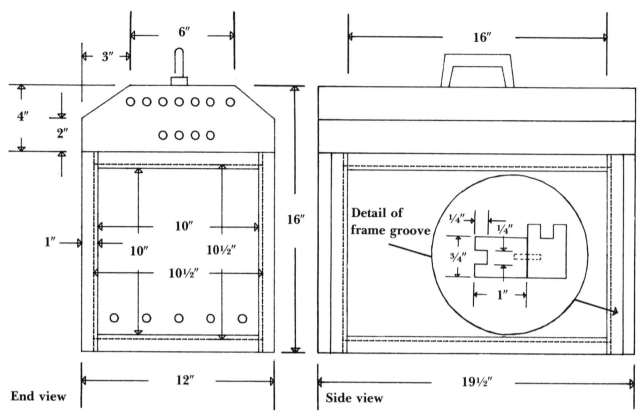

Illus. 6.29 Cat Carrier plans.

carrier is not extremely difficult to build, being primarily of plywood, though with framed sides and ends (Illus. 6.29).

Start construction by cutting the end and side pieces from the ¼-inch plywood. Cut the bottom piece from either ½-inch or ¾-inch plywood. Use this piece B side up. The bottom piece will be butt-jointed to the side and end panels, fitting inside once the frame is assembled, using glue and 6d nails.

The frame is the most complex part of the construction. Cut all the frame pieces and run a ¼-inch by ¼-inch dado down the length of each piece. Join the corners of the frame pieces using dowels. Make sure to position plywood inserts inside the frame pieces as you glue up the dowel joints.

Once the glue has dried on the frame assemblies, you are ready to biscuit-join ends to sides: the ends fit outside the longer sides. If you don't want to biscuit-join the joints, use screws, and glue, to make the joints. Align one end and a side around the bottom, and join to the bottom. Then use brass wood screws 1½ inches long if flat

head and countersunk, 2 inches if round headed, to make the joint. Glue is not essential here, but a few dabs of epoxy will offer greater security.

Materials

End and side panels: ¼″ plywood or OSB
two end panel pieces . . . . 10½″ × 10½″
two side panel pieces . . . . 16½″ × 10½″

Bottom: ½″ or ¾″ exterior plywood, B-C
one piece . . . . 16½″ × 10½″

Top frame: ¾″ stock, preferably oak or maple, 1″ wide
four side frame pieces . . . . 10″ lengths
four longer side frame pieces . . . . . 12″ lengths
four end pieces . . . . 12″ lengths
four longer end pieces . . . . 16″ lengths

Top panels: ½″ or ¾″ exterior plywood, B-C
one bevelled piece (75°) . . . . cut to fit
two pieces (60° bevel on one edge) . . . cut to fit
two middle pieces (60° both edges) . . . cut to fit

Top end plates: ½″ or ¾″ exterior plywood, B-C
two pieces . . . . cut to fit

The top is dimensioned to fit (Illus. 6.30), with the upper edge bevels cut at 75° and the lower edge bevels at 60°. The top is joined with epoxy and 2d galvanized finishing nails. End plates for the top are also cut to fit.

The handle is a commercial model, and is screwed onto the middle top.

Do not forget airholes. Your cat will now have a useful and comfortable, lightweight travelling case, which may be finished with enamel, or clear stains and polyurethane. The interior floor should have at least three coats of satin polyurethane over a coating or two of a polyurethane primer.

Illus. 6.30 Cutting plywood top to fit.

7
Small-Animal Needs and General Accessories

Enclosures are needed for keeping any number of small pets. Small cages come in handy for rabbits even if they have an open run area, and slightly smaller versions can be readily built for gerbils, hamsters, or snakes as well as similar pets. The enclosures presented here can be adapted to the needs of your small animal with little or no alteration. The projects for general accessories include ways to store your pet's equipment such as leashes or collars and places to store feed.

Hutch For Two Rabbits

This rabbit hutch allows access from two sides to separate compartments for full-sized rabbits (Illus. 7.1). The bottom of the hutch can be built as a solid base or covered with hardware mesh the same as the sides.

Begin construction by cutting the main pieces from the ¾-inch, B-C grade exterior plywood. Cut a bottom piece if you prefer the solid floor to the wire mesh. Cut the divider and a top piece, using solid wood for the top piece, as desired. Cut two lid pieces each 25 inches wide and at least 16⅝ inches deep, increasing the depth up to about 19 inches depending on the amount of overhang you would like. The top edge of each lid piece takes a bevel at 60°.

In cutting the end pieces, lay out the overall dimension of 36 inches wide by 24 inches high. Mark up 16 inches on both edges, and then measure in along the top 14½ inches from both edges so that you have a flat top in the middle measuring 7 inches across. Draw lines from the edges of this top down to the 16-inch marks along the edges, and cut the end pieces.

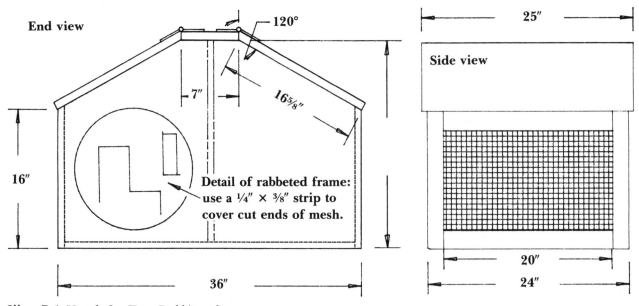

Illus. 7.1 Hutch for Two Rabbits, plans.

Materials

Bottom (as desired), divider, lids, ends: ¾″ exterior plywood, B-C
  one bottom piece . . . . 36″ × 24″
  one divider piece . . . . 22½″ × 22½″
  two lid pieces . . . . 25″ × 16⅝″ (minimum) to 19″
  two end pieces . . . . . . 36″ × 24″ (taper to 16″ at edges, 7″ wide top)

Top: ¾″ exterior plywood, B-C or solid wood, as desired
  one top piece . . . . 7″ × 24″

Side frames: one-by-three solid wood lumber
  four side pieces . . . . 15¼″ lengths
  four top and bottom pieces . . . . . . 20″ lengths
  mesh covering strips, ¼″ × ⅜″ . . . . . cut to fit

Divider supports (optional): two-by-two lumber

Finishing and assembly needs:
  ¼″ hardware mesh, cut to fit
  dowels or corner bracing plates
  4d galvanized finishing nails
  brass hinges, 3″ × 2″, and two sets of hook and eye
  paint or enamel (as desired) and clear polyurethane

Cut the pieces for the side frames from one-by-three lumber. On the top of each of the four side-edge pieces for the frame, cut a bevel at 30° to allow a flush closing of the lids.

Before you start assembling the frame pieces, mark the inside edge and back of each, and cut a ⅜-inch wide by 7/16-inch deep rabbet along the inside edges. Actually, if you plan things out carefully, you can cut the rabbet in the stock before you have cut each frame piece to size. The rabbet is necessary to allow room to staple the hardware mesh, yet be able to protect the rabbits from scraping and cutting themselves by covering the raw edge of the mesh with a smooth strip of wood.

Once the frame pieces are rabbetted, assemble each of the side frames by joining the corners of the boards with dowels or with corner brace plates of metal. The longer frame pieces butt against the outside

edge pieces. Check to make sure the bevels and rabbets face the right way before gluing up.

All of the pieces except the top and lids fit inside the end pieces. Assemble the end pieces up against the bottom piece, and place the middle divider. The divider can be supported with two-by-two pieces on both sides of the top and bottom if needed. Place the side frame assemblies, with the mesh and ¼-inch by ⅜-inch wood strips already in place, along with the top piece, and mark nailing lines (⅜ inch in for ¼-inch material). Use 4d galvanized finishing nails, and secure all the pieces.

Attach the lids using two 3-inch by 2-inch brass hinges for each lid. Use a hook and eye to keep each lid closed so that larger rabbits won't be able to push the cage open.

Coat the inside of the hutch with a clear polyurethane, either in satin or semigloss. If you built your hutch with the solid base, then apply at least three coats to this floor. Finish the outside according to your desires, with an outdoor paint or enamel.

Single Occupant Rabbit Hutch

I had occasion to build and use this handy easy-to-clean hutch when some time ago we rescued the baby rabbit Frances from the ravages of the lawn mower. The top, front, and bottom are all open frames covered with hardware mesh (Illus. 7.2). The back and ends are solid ½-inch plywood.

Materials

Back, ends: ½″ exterior plywood
  one back piece . . . . 24″ × 15¼″
  two end pieces . . . . 15¼″ square

Frame: 2″ or wider white pine, ¾″ thickness
  two top pieces, mitred 45° . . . . 24″ lengths
  two top pieces, mitred 45° . . . . 16″ lengths
  front side pieces, two . . . . 15¼″ lengths
  front cross pieces, two . . . . 20″ lengths

Floor frame: one-by-one material
  frame for mesh . . . . 22½″ × 14¾″
  cleats for floor frame, one-by-one material

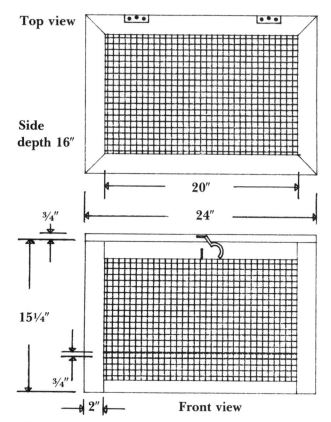

Top view

Side
depth 16"

3/4"

15¼"

3/4"

20"

24"

2"

Front view

Illus. 7.2 Single Occupant Rabbit Hutch, plans.

Start construction by cutting out the pieces for the back and ends—you can also cut a piece for a solid bottom if you prefer that to the open mesh of the design.

Cut the frame pieces for the top to length and then cut 45 mitres on each end. Cut the four front frame pieces, leaving the ends square. Before assembling these top and front frame pieces, be sure you cut a rabbet along the inside edge of each that is 7/16 inch wide by 3/8 inch deep. You can also cut the rabbet before you cut the pieces to length.

Assemble the front frame piece by butt-joining the long pieces inside of the shorter edge pieces. Staple in the hardware mesh, and cover that with the ¼-inch by 3/8-inch strips to keep it from snagging on the rabbit. Also assemble the top mitred frame, adding the mesh and applying the strips.

Put together the back and end pieces with the front frame, nailing the back and the front to the ends. Measure up from the base of the edges about three or four inches and mark. Cut and install one-by-one cleats on which the floor frame (or solid piece) will be nailed.

Construct the frame for the floor from one-by-one material to an outer dimension of 22½ inches by 14¾ inches. Staple wire hardware mesh to the floor frame, and nail the floor assembly to the already prepared cleats (Illus. 7.3).

Attach the mitred top frame, with mesh already in place, using 2-inch by 1-inch solid brass hinges (Illus. 7.4). The lid is held in place by a small hook and eye.

To finish the enclosure, you can choose from painting, staining, or simply coating all the wood with an exterior polyurethane. The cage I made was left unfinished, since we kept it indoors mostly. But, now it also stands unused because baby Frances grew up. We released him as soon as he seemed big enough to adapt back to the wild.

Illus. 7.3 The hutch bottom, stapled to one-by-one stock and nailed to cleats.

Illus. 7.4 Surface mount brass hinges work best.

Hamster or Snake Cage

This is a handy dual-purpose—but, please, not at the same time—cage (Illus. 7.5) that is very similar to the single occupant rabbit hutch above. Here, instead of the wire hardware mesh, the design uses glass or plastic (plastic is preferable by far).

Materials

Floor: ¾″ exterior or pressure-treated plywood, B-C

    one floor piece (laminate, if desired) . . . . 22½″ × 14¾″

Back, ends: ½″ exterior plywood
    one back piece . . . . 24″ × 15¼″
    two end pieces . . . . 15¼″ square

Frame: one-by-three pine (cut down to 2″ or left at 2½″)
    two top pieces, mitred 45° . . . . 24″ lengths
    two top pieces, mitred 45° . . . . 16″ lengths
    front side pieces, two . . . . 15¼″ lengths
    front cross pieces, two 20″ (2″ width) or 19″ (2½″ width)

Begin constructing the cage by cutting out the plywood pieces. Cut the ¾-inch floor piece, the ½-inch back, and both end pieces.

The front and top are framed in white pine, with the front butt-jointed and the top mitred. Start with one-by-three lumber, and either use the actual width as is at 2½ inches or cut down the stock to a 2-inch actual thickness. The white pine pieces are also grooved along their length to allow the plastic or tempered glass to nest securely in the frame. You may prefer to cut the ¼-inch deep (⅜-inch for medium-sized snakes) groove into the stock before cutting the frame pieces to size. In either case, cut the groove to the proper width that suits the particular plastic or glass thickness being used. I suggest a ¼-inch thickness or at least ³⁄₁₆ of an inch. Tempered glass is especially important if the cage is to be used for snakes.

Cut the frame pieces to size, and according to the width chosen. Mitre the top frame

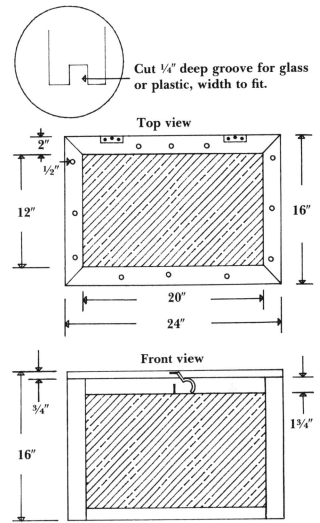

Cut ¼″ deep groove for glass or plastic, width to fit.

Illus. 7.5 Hamster or Snake Cage, plans.

pieces, and drill air holes, as shown in Illus. 7.5. For very slender snakes, the breathing holes can be easily increased, while being reduced from a ½-inch diameter to ¼ inch. The bottom edge of the floor could also have air holes drilled, as desired.

Start the assembly with the frames, placing the plastic or glass in the grooves provided. Butt-joint the front frame, and mitre-joint the top frame. The floor sits inside the front, back, and ends. Place the floor with the B side up, and nail the assemblies to it, with the end pieces fitting inside the front assembly and the back.

With the box part together, place the lid and attach the two solid brass hinges. To complete the cage, add a hook and eye to the front to secure the lid and finish with paint, stain, or polyurethane, as desired.

Dry Food Holder

This food holder is easy to make and more attractive than bags or boxes (Illus. 7.6). The visible portions are all made of solid wood, enhancing the appealing character of this simple piece. It can be made rodent proof with either sheet aluminum or sheet steel (tin-plated) lining. If rodents are a problem in your area, look around (in weekly newspapers, etc.) for an establishment selling used printing plates. These plates are aluminum, and especially make good mouse-proofing when used as liners (cats will give their all to the effort, but some things—like the food supply—need extra measures).

Start construction by cutting the front, top, lid, and bottom pieces. Now begin laying out the side pieces by measuring 26 inches and marking two pieces 10½-inches wide. Mark a top portion 3-inches wide, and draw a line from there down to a 20-inch high mark. Cut that taper on both boards, as shown (Illus. 7.6).

All of the preparation for joining the many pieces is done only on the side pieces. To allow the sides to accept the back piece, cut a ¼-inch by ⅜-inch deep dado along

Materials

Back: ¼" hardboard, OSB, or plywood
one back piece . . . . 25½" × 19½"

Front, top, lid: ¾" × 11" solid pine
one front piece . . . . 20" × 11"
one top piece . . . . 3" × 11"
one lid piece . . . . 11½" × 10½"

Bottom, sides: ¾" × 10½" solid pine
one bottom piece . . . . 9½" × 10¾"
two side pieces . . . . 10½" × 26" overall,
with 3"-wide top tapering to 20" high front

the back edge of both side pieces. To accept the bottom piece, cut a ¾-inch by ⅜-inch dado along the lower edge of both side pieces. And, to accept the front piece and top, run a ¾-inch rabbet, ¼-inch deep, along the front edge of each side piece and along the top. The bottom is butt-jointed front and back.

Glue and nail the pieces together, checking for square as you go. Position the lid and attach the two cabinet hinges. Add any mouse-proofing that you feel is needed, and then stain to suit and finish with tung oil or polyurethane.

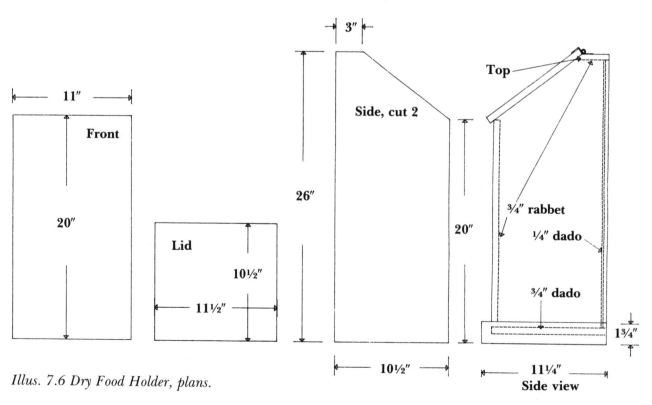

Illus. 7.6 Dry Food Holder, plans.

Equipment Box

This dovetailed solid-wood equipment box (Illus. 7.7) provides not only an attractive piece of furniture, but also a useful place to store any kind of pet paraphernalia that you would rather keep out of sight, from combs and brushes to spare leashes, temporarily unused toys, and flea sprays. The box is assembled as a closed, nonopening box, which is then cut on your table saw to yield a top piece and the bottom section of the box. The final box also has an inner tray. You will need to glue-up edge-joined lumber to have sufficient width for the pieces.

Glue-up a sufficient length of stock to cover the widths needed. Cut a ½-inch by ⅜-inch deep rabbet along one edge either before or after cutting the front, back, and end pieces to length. The rabbet will accept the ½″ plywood bottom, which should be cut 29¼ inches by 17¼ inches. Also cut the top piece from glued-up stock to yield a size of 28½ inches by 16½ inches.

Set up your dovetailing jig—the Keller medium-sized dovetail jig suits this plan perfectly. You can cut the slots for the handle holes (if desired) either before or after cutting the dovetails, but before assembly. Dovetail the ends of each of the side pieces.

Materials

Ends, front, back, top: glued-up solid wood
   two end pieces, dovetailed . . . . 18″ × 18″
   front and back pieces, dovetailed . . . 30″ × 10″
   one top piece . . . . 28½″ × 16½″

Bottom of box: ½″ plywood
   one piece . . . . 29¼″ × 17¼″

Sides of inner tray: ½″ × 2″ solid wood
   front and back sides . . . . 28½″ lengths
   end pieces . . . . 15½″ lengths

Bottom of inner tray: ¼″ plywood
   one piece . . . . 28″ × 16″

Cleats for tray: ¾″ × 1″ (actual) pieces cut to fit

Assemble the box—the inner tray will be added at the finish. The bottom piece fits in the rabbet along the bottom edge of the side pieces. The top piece sets in flush with simple butt joints all the way around. Assembled in this manner, the box is a single, nonopening unit. Set your table saw for a depth of cut of one inch, and set your rip fence to 16 inches. Cut the top two inches of the box loose, being very careful to slip kerf supports into the cut as you move

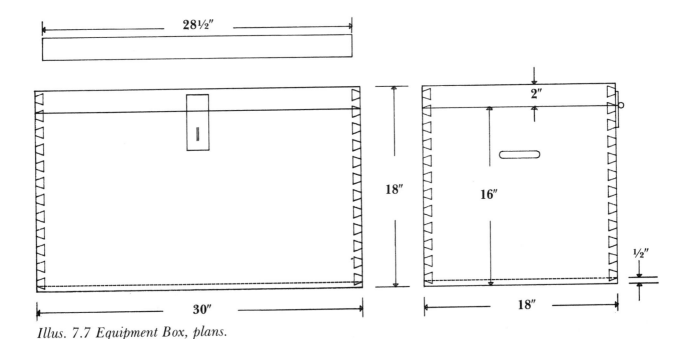

Illus. 7.7 Equipment Box, plans.

around the box. The safest way to protect your work while making this cut is to place each kerf support and immediately apply masking tape to keep the supported cut securely closed.

Once the top is free from the lower section of the box, reattach this top lid with brass hinges, and add a brass hasp to close the front. Cut side pieces for the inner tray, making sure the measurements are adjusted for the actual box, and cut a tray bottom from ¼-inch plywood so that it will fit in ¼-inch by ¼-inch rabbets cut into the tray sides. Cut the side rabbets, and assemble the tray.

Measure and cut ¾-inch thick by 1-inch cleats to support the tray all the way around the inside of the box. Glue and screw the cleats in place. If you have used pine or fir, stain the completed box. Finish with satin or flat polyurethane for the best and most appropriate look.

Leash and Collar Board

This leash and collar board (Illus. 7.8) can be extremely handy once you select a convenient place, and wall-mount it with flat or

Materials

Mounting board: solid wood, oak, pine, cherry, etc.
one piece .14″ × 3½″

Pegs: Shaker (larger) and tee, or key (smaller) pegs
three larger pegs
two smaller pegs

round head wood screws. Construction couldn't be simpler, and assembly is very rapid with some time allowed for glue and finish to dry.

First, select a suitable piece of oak, pine, cherry, or other solid wood. By all means feel free to use a piece left over from another project even if the piece does not match exactly the dimensions given in the plan (Illus. 7.8). You may notice in the photographs that this is precisely how I came up with the piece of oak I used. Second, select Shaker, tee (or key), or other pegs.

Cut coves into the board—the edging pattern you select may simply depend on what router bits you have on hand (Illus. 7.9). Measure the diameters of the shaft (dowel)

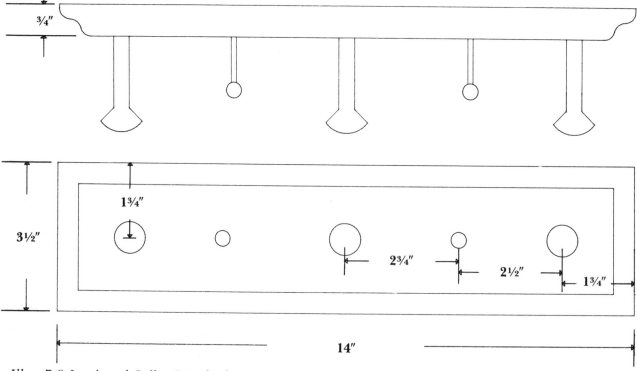

Illus. 7.8 Leash and Collar Board, plans.

part of your selected pegs (Illus. 7.10). Lay out the centers of the holes to be drilled in the mounting board (Illus. 7.11). Drill the holes for the dowels to the needed depth for each peg (Illus. 7.12). Add glue, insert the dowels, and tap the pegs securely into place (Illus. 7.13). Set the assembly aside for a day.

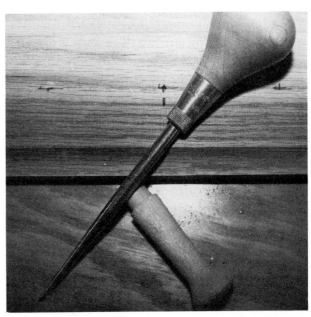

Illus. 7.11 Use a scribe to mark and center punch for the holes to be drilled.

Illus. 7.9 Oak board, with edges moulded on the router table.

Illus. 7.12 Drill the board to the appropriate depth.

Illus. 7.10 Measure dowel diameters before drilling. Lay out the marks.

Illus. 7.13 Glue the pegs in the board. I used hide glue, but you may wish to use another type.

A day later, come back and clean up the assembly, scraping off any excess glue. To finish the project, I applied some white oak stain to my oak board and the pegs, and then later I used four coats of spray polyurethane in a satin finish (Illus. 7.14).

Now all that is left is to drill two holes through the mounting board and into the wall at the spot you have selected. Use brass screws to add to the attractiveness of a simple, but useful, peg board.

Illus. 7.14 The board is stained before the final finishing.

Two Bin, Tip-Out Dog Food Holder

This food holder is for the person with more than one dog or a dog that likes—and gets—more than one kind of dried food (Illus. 7.15). The tip-out bins are easier to fill, reach into, and dump when needed than the usual lift-off top container or other drawer arrangement.

Place a screwed-in wooden stop at the top sides of the bin frame, or one turnable stop screwed to the back of the bin, to keep bins from tilting too far out, and for easy removal for cleaning, etc.

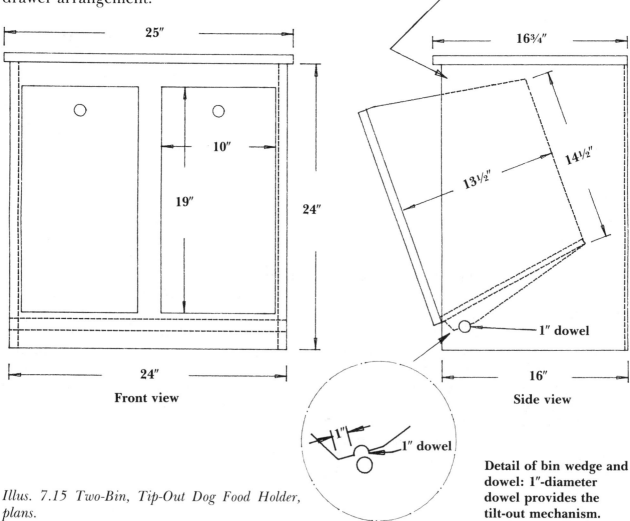

Front view

Side view

Detail of bin wedge and dowel: 1″-diameter dowel provides the tilt-out mechanism.

Illus. 7.15 Two-Bin, Tip-Out Dog Food Holder, plans.

Materials

Front frame: ¾″-thick pine stock
 two side pieces . . . . 1″ wide × 19″ length
 middle piece . . . . 2″ wide × 19″ length
 top piece . . . . 2″ wide × 24″ length
 bottom piece . . . . 3″ wide × 24″ length

Top: ¾″ glued-up pine
 one piece . . . . 16¾″ × 25″

Cabinet sides: ½″ or thicker plywood, B-C
 two side pieces . . . . 16″ × 24″

Cabinet back: ¼″ hardboard, OSB, or plywood
 one back piece . . . . 24″ × 23½″

Bin fronts: ¾″ glued-up solid stock, or plywood
 two front pieces . . . . 10″ × 19″ (minimum, + 1″ each for ½″ lip)

Bin sides, backs, bottoms: ½″ or thicker plywood,
 B-C
 four side pieces . . . . 13½″ × 14½″,
  widening to 19″ front
 two back pieces . . . . 14½″ × 9″
 two bottom pieces . . . . 13″ × 9″

Tapered bottom tilt-out pieces:
 four tapered pieces . . . . 13″ × 1½″ (at
  highest), taper to zero

Mounted wood stops: one-by-one lumber, 3″
 length

Cut all of the front frame pieces to size from the ¾-inch pine stock. Rabbet outside edges of the two one-inch wide side pieces to a width of ½ inch and a depth of ⅜ inch. Assemble the frame unit using dowels or flat brace plates.

Cut the two cabinet side pieces, and rabbet along the back 24-inch edge of each piece, ¼ inch by ¼ inch. Cut the cabinet back from ¼-inch material so that it will set into the side rabbets. Assemble the front frame, the cabinet sides and the cabinet back. Holes for the dowel-tilting mecha-

nism can be drilled before this assembly stage, or later once the bins have been fully constructed. They are one-inch holes.

Cut the bin fronts, adding to the dimensions, as desired, to increase the overhang on the frame. At least a one-half inch overhang is recommended. Cut the bin sides, backs, and bottoms, being careful especially to lay out the sides so that the taper from 19 inches in the front to 14½ inches in the back is uniform, above and below. Groove these pieces as required, making sure that the direction of load or pull will be against wood, and not against glue or nails alone. If a straight plowed groove is used, a ¾-inch thick strip should be glued and nailed for support along the groove. The sides are then nailed into this backer board as well as glued into the groove. The bottom piece fits inside the back and front of each bin. In all cases, place the B side of the plywood in, for a smooth surface.

Assemble the bins using 2d galvanized nails and glue. Cut and add a tapered bottom tilt-out piece to each side of both bins. Glue and screw these in place, with a one-inch diameter arc cut out to fit over the one-inch dowel-tilting mechanism. Place a wooden stop at the top front of the cabinet frame, on the outside, screwed in to keep the bins from tilting too far out. Alternatively, you can mount a block with a single screw to each of the backs of the bins so that the block can be twisted up to block the bin from tilting out or twisting horizontally to allow easy removal of the bins for cleaning, or moving.

Install the bins. Cut a top cabinet piece from glued-up lumber, and attach the top to the frame with glue and screws.

To complete the dog food holder, mount a wooden drawer-pull knob, centered about 3 inches down from the top edges of the bins, on the front of each bin. Finish the piece as desired.

8
Finishing

With some projects, it may well seem that the most important part is finishing. Certainly with most of the projects finishing is an essential element to making the piece complete. Without the appropriate finish, exterior projects simply do not last very long. Without finishing, projects that are displayed and used indoors are not particularly attractive—and durability is lessened, because surfaces can more easily show wear from scratches and general exposure to household incidents.

There are, basically, two types of finishes for any of these projects, opaque and clear. Opaque finishes include paints, and both semitransparent and opaque stains, while clear finishes include varnishes, shellacs, polyurethanes, and tung oils as well as the underlying transparent stains that enhance wood color and emphasize wood grains.

Opaque Finishes

Today, any worries about lead being a component of an opaque finish are minimal. Most finishes are safe for use with pets that might chew on certain areas of the project from time to time.

Depending on the qualities needed, you'll find plenty of opaque finishes that will produce good work. Ordinary house paints do as well on doghouses and cat abodes as they do on human homes. Opaque and semitransparent stains can offer great coverage, while, especially in humid areas, offering a more permeable pigment coat. This means there is less chance that the coating will peel from a build-up of water beneath its surface (Illus. 8.1).

General preparation is the same as ever. Sand surfaces lightly—rough wood may need planing and heavy sanding, unless you prefer retaining the rough texture. Apply the coating with the widest suitable brush, using as few brush strokes as possible.

If more than one coat is needed, make sure the underlying coat is dry. Most finishes will indicate on the label that recoating can take place within a specific number of hours. Take that as a minimum, and remember that under some weather conditions, you're far better off allowing the first coat alone an extra twelve or even twenty-four hours. If your area is extremely humid, give all of the coatings extra drying time before sanding, or recoating. Other-

Illus. 8.1 Opaque stains make excellent exterior finishes and clean up easily, after going on with a minimum of brushing. Note that the brush is meant for use with water-based products.

wise, apply coatings according to the manufacturer's directions, using a good quality brush. Most coatings today are latex—water—based, so natural bristle brushes do not work as well as synthetic bristle kinds.

In virtually all cases, coatings should be applied to both sides of the project to prevent unequal water gain and loss, which would otherwise create warping where there need be none.

Clear Finishes

As a nonpurist, I have little use for shellacs and similar finishes that require hours of work to produce a finish that looks about the same as that acquired in minutes using tung oils or polyurethanes. While there are some minor advantages in using shellacs, lacquers, and nonpolyurethane varnishes, those are usually significantly offset by the susceptibility of the resulting finish to damage from water—or from chemicals—and by the inherent difficulty in laying on the finish properly, no matter what the technique used.

Stains go on easily if they're not water based (Illus. 8.2). Water-based stains raise the grain in wood, making you come back and cut off the raised grain using a scraper, steel wool, or sandpaper, depending on your preference. Standard oil stains do not raise the grain, and penetrate about the same.

In general, it is a good idea to use stains and coatings from the same maker, though not essential. If you are using finishing products from different makers, test the coating over the stain before doing the entire finishing job. Use a 6-inch by 6-inch wood scrap to discover problems rather than the entire project.

For clear finishes, more care is usually taken to get a good finished look, as mistakes tend to show up far more readily than with paints and opaque stains (Illus. 8.3). Thus, wood preparation is particularly important.

Start by checking to see just how smooth the finished wood is. If it is about normal, start sanding with a 120 grit sandpaper, and progress from there to a 180 grit. For maple and similar woods, that's usually sufficient. For more-open-grained woods (oak, walnut, pine, etc.) go on to at least a 220 grit. To obtain a super-fine finish for oak and walnut (also hickory, pecan, and other open-grained hardwoods), go on to a filler and a 320 grit sandpaper.

Once that is done, the stain, if used, is easily applied with almost any soft rag, though cheesecloth or an old T-shirt is preferable. Allow the piece plenty of drying time.

Go over the stained surface lightly with 0000 steel wool, and then come back with a vacuum or a blow gun on an air compressor. After that, go over the entire project with a tack cloth to get up any embedded dust.

Unless the clear material used next is listed as a primer/sealer, you will want to reduce the first coat by 50 percent, using paint thinner or turpentine. Brush the first coat on gently. Clear finishes should not be

Illus. 8.2 Apply wood stain with a rag, wiping gently.

Illus. 8.3 Three types of clear wood finish: exterior polyurethane differs from interior by including ultraviolet inhibitors; stain and polyurethane includes finish-borne stain, while the others are more clear; quick dry polyurethane primer/sealer, which will provide a quick, low-gloss, polyurethane finish in a pinch, and in a rush.

stirred—or as little as possible—to prevent the creation of air bubbles. By the same token, the fewest brush strokes, and the gentler those strokes are, will also create fewer air bubbles to dry into the surface and create problems.

If the job is a fast one, you can lay on a moderately heavy second coat of polyurethane or tung oil after the preparatory coat has dried, and be reasonably satisfied.

For more durable—and attractive—finishes, you will want as many as five coats, total, of tung oil, polyurethane, or other varnishes. As an example, I start with a coat of ZAR Quick Dry polyurethane, and allow that to dry for at least eight hours. Normal drying time is only one hour on bare wood for the first application, but my shop is not a normally dry area, except in winter.

A light brushing with 0000 steel wool is followed by a dusting down with a tack cloth. Then the piece gets a second coat of Quick Dry, and at least twelve hours to dry (three hours in winter).

At this point, things may change. If I'm continuing with satin tung oil, I still cut its first coat 50 percent. If I'm using ZAR Antique Flat polyurethane, I put the first coat on full strength. Either way, six hours drying time seems to be more than enough to allow good drying for second-coat adhesion. A quick brush with a tack cloth is followed by its second coat.

That second coat gets at least twelve hours to dry, after which it is lightly cut with either 400 grit sandpaper, or 0000 steel wool. The third coat is the final coat for most applications (you will note that the third coat of these finishes is actually the fifth overall coat).

For a really deep finish, you may wish to add two or three more coats, again lightly using the 0000 steel wool between coats, and using a vacuum and tack cloth, or blow gun and tack cloth, to make sure the surface is dust free before coating.

For coating purposes, standard good-quality natural bristle brushes work well, *if* you make sure the bristles, and the paint thinner they're cleaned in, remain as dust free as the surface of the wood you're coating! Get dust on the brush, and you've got dust in the finish, just as if it were on the surface to start.

Using a Spray Gun

Both heavier (latex) materials and the light varnishes can be readily and easily applied with a spray gun (Illus. 8.4). There is some difference with each and every spray gun, and with compressors, but generally you will want as large a nozzle opening as possible with the heavy liquids, and as small a one as recommended with the lighter liquids—and most coatings, whatever their kind, will be thinned for use in spray guns.

Check the manufacturer's instructions for the spray gun, and the instructions for the material being sprayed. Keep the gun totally clean, and make sure there is a filter unit in the line between the gun and the compressor. If there isn't, eventually condensation from your tank is going to end up spitting out on the surface being finished and ruining the finish.

Illus. 8.4 Setting up to use a spray gun to apply a latex finish. The gas-driven compressor in this case was used close by, as the entire project was outdoors. For indoor use, simply leave the compressor outdoors and run the hose indoors to the spray gun. For outdoor use, make sure you do the finish work on a day of light or no wind, or find some means of keeping the wind off the project.

Appendix A

Some Useful Woods

Wood	Locale	Characteristics
Ash	East of Rockies in U.S.	Strong, heavy, tough grain that is straight. Sometimes substitutes for more costly oaks.
Basswood	Eastern half of U.S.	Soft, light, weak wood that shrinks considerably. Very uniform, works easily, does not twist or warp.
Beech	East of Mississippi in U.S., southeastern Canada	Similar to birch, shrinks, checks considerably, close grain, may be a light or dark red color.
Birch	East of Mississippi, north of Gulf Coast states in U.S., southeast Canada, Newfoundland	Hard, durable, fine grain, even texture, heavy and stiff, as well as strong, works easily, takes a high polish. Heartwood is light to dark reddish brown.
Butternut	Southern Canada, Minnesota, eastern U.S., to Alabama, Florida	Much like walnut, but is softer. Not as soft as white pine and basswood, easy to work, fairly strong.
Cherry	Eastern U.S.	Superb working close-grained furniture wood. Reddish color, darkens with age if not stained. Durable, strong, easy to machine.
Cypress	Maryland to Texas, U.S.	Resembles white cedar, water-resistant, very durable. May be expensive and difficult to locate.
Douglas fir	Pacific Coast of U.S. and British Columbia in Canada	Strong, light, clear-grained, tends to brittleness. Heartwood somewhat resistant to weathering, available, moderately priced, but rising in recent years.
Elm	East of Colorado in U.S.	Slippery, heavy, hard, tough, difficult to split, durable.
Hickory	Arkansas, Tennessee, Ohio, Kentucky in U.S.	Very heavy, hard, tough. Strongest and toughest of our native hardwoods. Checks, shrinks, difficult to work.
Lignum vitae	Central America	Dark greenish-brown wood. Usually hard, close grained, exceptionally heavy, hard to work, characterized by a soapy feel. Useful for mallets, etc.
Live oak	Coasts of Oregon, California, southern Atlantic and Gulf states in U.S.	Heavy, hard, strong, durable. A bear to work, but superb for small projects otherwise.
Mahogany	Honduras, Mexico, Central America, Florida in U.S., West Indies, Central Africa	Brown to red color, one of the top cabinet woods. Hard, durable, does not split badly, open grained, but checks, swells, shrinks, warps slightly.
Maple	All U.S. states east of Colorado, southern Canada	Heavy, tough, strong, easy to work, not durable. May be costly. Rock, or sugar, maple is the hardest.

Norway pine	U.S. states along Great Lakes	Light-colored, moderately hard for softwood, not durable, easy to work.
Poplar	Virginia, W. Virginia, Kentucky, along Mississippi Valley in U.S.	Soft, cheap hardwood, good for wide boards—tree grows fast and straight—rots quickly if not protected, works easily. Warps, brittle, fine texture.
Red cedar	East of Colorado, north of Florida in U.S.	Very light, very soft, weak, brittle wood, works easily. May be hard to find in wide boards, very durable.
Red oak	Virginia, W. Virginia, Kentucky, Tenn., Arkansas, Ohio, Missouri, Maryland, parts of New York in U.S.	Coarse grained, easily warped and not durable. Forget for outdoor uses.
Redwood	California in U.S.	Ideal construction and durability characteristics. Tends to higher cost, not as strong as yellow pine, but shrinks and splits little, is straight-grained, exceptionally durable with no finish at all. Many inexpensive grades available, and possibly suitable.
Spruce	New York, New England, W. Virginia, Great Lakes states, Idaho, Washington, Oregon in U.S., much of central Canada	Light, soft, fairly durable wood that is close to ideal for outdoor projects.
Sugar pine	California, Oregon in U.S.	Very light, soft, resembles white pine closely.
Walnut	Eastern half of U.S., some in New Mexico, Arizona, California	Fine furniture wood, considered by many to be the ultimate. Coarse grained, but takes superb finish when pores are filled. Durable, brittle, modest shrinkage, often knotty.
White cedar	Eastern coast of the U.S., around Great Lakes	Soft, light, durable wood, close-grained, excellent for outdoor uses.
White oak	Virginia, W. Virginia, Tenn., Arkansas, Ohio, Kentucky, Missouri, Maryland, Indiana in U.S.	Heavy, hard, strong, moderately coarse grain. Tough, dense, most durable of all native American hardwoods, reasonably easy to work (with sharp tools). Tendency to shrink, crack, may be costly in some locales.
White pine	Minnesota, Wisconsin, Maine, Michigan, Idaho, Montana, Oregon, Washington, California, some stands in eastern U.S. other than Maine	Fine grained, easily worked, sometimes found with few knots. Durable, soft, not exceptionally strong, economical, excellent for many uses. White in color, shrinks, does not split easily.
Yellow pine	Virginia to Texas in U.S., some species classed as southern pine	Hard, tough softwood. Heartwood is fairly durable, hard to nail, saws and generally works easily, inexpensive, excellent for outdoor uses. Grain variable, reddish brown in color, heavy for a softwood, resinous.

Appendix B

Softwood Lumber Grades

Adapted from chart by the Southern Forest Products Association

Product	Grade	Character
Finish	B&B	Highest grade, generally clear, limited number of pin knots allowed. Natural or stain finish.
	C	Excellent for paint, or natural with lower needs. Limited number surface checks and small, tight knots allowed.
	C&Btr	Combination of above 2 grades.
	D	Economical, serviceable for natural or painted finish.
Boards S4S	1	High quality, good appearance. Sound and tight-knotted, largest hole permitted 1/16". Forms, shelving, crating.
	2	High quality sheathing. Tight knots, mostly free of holes.
	3	Good, serviceable sheathing.
	4	Pieces like No. 3, but below, with usable lengths at least 24". A useful grade for our purposes.
Dimension structural light framing 2"–4" thick 2"–4" wide	Select Structural, Dense select Structural	High quality, reasonably free of strength defects.
	1 & 1 Dense	High strength, general use, good appearance, limited knots.
	2 & 2 Dense	Not as good as No. 1, still for all construction. Tight knots.
	3 & 3 Dense	High quality, low cost, appearance not as good as No. 2, may be limited by single factor.
Studs 2"–4" thick 2"–6" wide 10' or shorter	Stud	Stringent requirements as to straightness, strength, stiffness, for all stud uses, including load bearing walls. Good for a lot of pet housing purposes.
Light framing 2"–4" thick 2"–4" wide	Construction	For general framing purposes. Appearance is good, strong, serviceable.
	Standard	Same uses as above, but allows larger defects.
	Utility	For blocking, plate, braces.
	Economy	Similar to Utility, but with shorter usable lengths, best used where strength, appearance are not critical.

Appendix C

Classification of various hardwood and softwood species according to gluing properties

	Hardwoods	Softwoods
Group 1		
Glues very easily with glues of wide range in properties and under a wide range of gluing conditions.	Aspen Chestnut, American Cottonwood Willow, black Poplar, yellow	Baldcypress Fir: White Grand Noble Pacific silver Calif. red Larch, western Redcedar, western Redwood Spruce, Sitka
Group 2		
Glues well with glues of fairly wide range in properties under a moderately wide range of gluing conditions.	Alder, red Basswood Butternut Elm: American and rock Hackberry Magnolia Mahogany Sweetgum	Douglas fir Hemlock, Western Pine: Eastern white Southern Ponderosa Redcedar, eastern
Group 3		
Glue satisfactorily with good quality glue under well controlled gluing conditions.	Ash, white Cherry, black Dogwood Maple, soft Oak: red white Pecan Sycamore Tupelo: black water Walnut, black	Alaska cedar
Group 4		
Require very close control of glue and gluing conditions, or special treatment, to obtain the best results.	Beech, American Birch, sweet and yellow Hickory Maple, hard Osage orange Persimmon	

Metric Conversion

INCHES TO MILLIMETRES AND CENTIMETRES

MM—millimetres   *CM—centimetres*

Inches	MM	CM	Inches	CM	Inches	CM
1/8	3	0.3	9	22.9	30	76.2
1/4	6	0.6	10	25.4	31	78.7
3/8	10	1.0	11	27.9	32	81.3
1/2	13	1.3	12	30.5	33	83.8
5/8	16	1.6	13	33.0	34	86.4
3/4	19	1.9	14	35.6	35	88.9
7/8	22	2.2	15	38.1	36	91.4
1	25	2.5	16	40.6	37	94.0
1¼	32	3.2	17	43.2	38	96.5
1½	38	3.8	18	45.7	39	99.1
1¾	44	4.4	19	48.3	40	101.6
2	51	5.1	20	50.8	41	104.1
2½	64	6.4	21	53.3	42	106.7
2	76	7.6	22	55.9	43	109.2
3½	89	8.9	23	58.4	44	111.8
4	102	10.2	24	61.0	45	114.3
4½	114	11.4	25	63.5	46	116.8
5	127	12.7	26	66.0	47	119.4
6	152	15.2	27	68.6	48	121.9
7	178	17.8	28	71.1	49	124.5
8	203	20.3	29	73.7	50	127.0

Index